Voices OF WOMEN OF THE *Cloth*

Voices of WOMEN of the Cloth

Best wishes to Nancy—

CLAIRE COLE CURCIO

Claire Cole Curcio

Copyright © 2017 Claire Cole Curcio.

All rights reserved. No part of this book may be used or reproduced by any means, graphic, electronic, or mechanical, including photocopying, recording, taping or by any information storage retrieval system without the written permission of the author except in the case of brief quotations embodied in critical articles and reviews.

Archway Publishing books may be ordered through booksellers or by contacting:

Archway Publishing
1663 Liberty Drive
Bloomington, IN 47403
www.archwaypublishing.com
1 (888) 242-5904

Because of the dynamic nature of the Internet, any web addresses or links contained in this book may have changed since publication and may no longer be valid. The views expressed in this work are solely those of the author and do not necessarily reflect the views of the publisher, and the publisher hereby disclaims any responsibility for them.

Any people depicted in stock imagery provided by Thinkstock are models, and such images are being used for illustrative purposes only. Certain stock imagery © Thinkstock.

ISBN: 978-1-4808-3808-6 (sc)
ISBN: 978-1-4808-3810-9 (hc)
ISBN: 978-1-4808-3809-3 (e)

Library of Congress Control Number: 2016919076

Print information available on the last page.

Archway Publishing rev. date: 12/6/2016

DEDICATION

Once again, thanks to my family for their belief in me

and

to all the amazing women who agreed to be interviewed

and most of all,

to my partner Selby, who listened, critiqued, read,
edited and encouraged every word in this book.

I was inspired to write *Voices of Women of the Cloth* by being friends with some of the women in this book before I undertook the writing. They were such an interesting group that I became curious to know more about how women decided to dedicate themselves to a religious life as a career.

Acknowledgements and Thanks

Several people were very helpful as I conceived the idea of this book and set about interviewing women. The Rev. Pam Webb helped develop the interview guide that loosely shaped the conversations that produced the data. Dr. Karen Scanlon recommended Roman Catholic sisters and then helped interpret information after the interviews. Penny Perry assisted me in finding a young woman to interview to give a broader view of experience by age. The Rev. Kent Rahm and Jim Carlock of Trinity Episcopal Church in Fredericksburg, VA, recommended women who would be interesting to interview.

A group of friends and family spent significant time reading the manuscript and making helpful suggestions, including: Lt. Col. Scott Cole (Ret.), Dr. June Hall McCash, Steve Cole, Rosemary Powley Cole, and Ronda Worcester. Members of my writing group, the Water Street Writers of Fredericksburg, VA, made excellent suggestions, especially helping me get the professorial wording out of the manuscript. My women's book group at Trinity Episcopal Church encouraged me all the way and voted to discuss the book even before it was published, a true act of faith!

My wonderful editor, Emily Carmain of Noteworthy Editing

Services, provided invaluable technical advice and encouraging comments.

Each woman interviewed in the book has read and approved the content of her own chapter.

Contents

Introduction		xi
CHAPTER 1	Clergywomen in America	1
CHAPTER 2	Pam	7
CHAPTER 3	Melva	18
CHAPTER 4	Michele and Monique	30
CHAPTER 5	Cathie	41
CHAPTER 6	Sarah	54
CHAPTER 7	Brenda	61
CHAPTER 8	Torrence	70
CHAPTER 9	Tanya	82
CHAPTER 10	Gaye	91
CHAPTER 11	Jann	101
CHAPTER 12	Margaret	111
CHAPTER 13	Kate	120
CHAPTER 14	Donna	129
CHAPTER 15	Mary	137
CHAPTER 16	Betsy	148

CHAPTER 17	Sister Miriam Elizabeth	159
CHAPTER 18	Christine	165
CHAPTER 19	Amy	175
CHAPTER 20	Amazing Women!	184
APPENDIX A	Denominational Ordination of Women	192
APPENDIX B	Denominational Ordination History	194
Sources Cited or Consulted		200

Introduction

My own theological history is either ecumenical or scattered, depending on your perspective. My mother attended a small fundamental church and my father was a lapsed Roman Catholic, really an anti-Catholic by the time I entered the world. I began my church life sitting on my maternal grandmother's lap in a small church building in rural Missouri, being fed peppermints by my Nanny to bribe me to sit still during the service. My Grampy sat with the other men in another part of the church building.

Women had no part in leading the church service, nor was there any instrumental music or mention of the Old Testament that I can recall. Some Sundays it took a lot of peppermints to get me through the interminable services. The last time I attended that church in the same little town a few years ago, things didn't appear to have changed much.

The journey from that small fundamental New Testament church to serving on the vestry at Trinity Episcopal Church in Fredericksburg, VA, has included growing up in the Presbyterian Church in Manassas, VA, and many good years of membership in Blacksburg Presbyterian and Northside Presbyterian where I was an ordained elder in Blacksburg, VA. I spent a short stint in the Vaught family pew of the Rural Retreat (VA) United Methodist

Church, my husband Jim Vaught's family church, and in the Luther Memorial Lutheran Church in Blacksburg.

I'm not quite sure how we ended up Lutheran, but I remember Jim saying, "You'll like it here, they sing a lot," as he swung into the parking lot one Sunday morning when I'd thought we were on our way to the Presbyterian Church. And he was right. It was a church filled with joy and warmth. When my devastatingly short marriage to Jim ended with his sudden death, the wonderful church we attended together was too lonely to attend by myself, despite their best efforts to befriend me.

I married Charlie Curcio, a Roman Catholic, a few years later and we found our way to Episcopal churches in Blacksburg, in Ormond Beach, FL, and finally to Trinity in Fredericksburg. Trinity is the most service-oriented church I have ever attended and when I was again a widow, I felt very much at home there. My partner, Selby McCash—I call him an "agnostic Quaker"—and I are now very active in that church.

I decided to write this book because I have several strong, wonderful clergywomen friends and I remain in awe of their dedication, wisdom, and perseverance in their chosen career. I wanted to know more about their stories. A major interest in my own work life was career counseling and it intrigued me to know how these women had made their decisions and attained their career credentials.

The older I get, as with many other people, the more I become interested in spiritual matters. If I were younger, I might have gone to seminary myself, not to become a clergywoman but to learn all I could about theology. Lacking the stamina and internal drive to do that these days, and likely lacking a seminary that would admit a septuagenarian, I decided to do these interviews as a way of learning for myself.

For the first fifty or so years of my life, I knew no clergywomen. I did not attend a church myself that had female clergy until the 1990s. The Lutheran church in Blacksburg had (and still has) a very fine female associate pastor. The Reverend Clare Fischer-Davies, a wonderful Episcopal priest at Christ Church in Blacksburg, married Charlie and me in 2001. There have been two assistant female rectors in the twelve years I've attended Trinity in Fredericksburg. Of the twenty-five or so pastors whose churches I've belonged to, all major denominations, only four were women, and only one of those was senior pastor.

And learn I have from writing this book. I discovered that it's pretty difficult to locate up-to-date data on female clergy. For example, one recent study on stress in the clergy included only men. The last chapter will summarize some of the things I've learned about clergywomen from these interviews.

Along the way writing this book I have met some amazing women and made some new friends. I enjoy time with one as we meet for an occasional weekend of conversation, exchange frequent emails with some of the women in the book, and have a cup of coffee now and then with some others.

My eyes and mind have opened to new ways of looking at spiritual matters. Almost every woman I interviewed either handed me a book to read or pointed me toward one, so my theological reading has taken many new directions.

Wanting to do the interviews in person, I found interesting women to talk to in Virginia, North Carolina, Pennsylvania and Georgia. All of them were designated chaplains, ministers or sisters, but right away that became an unclear issue. What is a clergywoman, anyway? I first decided that meant someone ordained as a minister. However, I later expanded the definition to include those who led a church or were called minister, pastor, or chaplain, or who belonged to a Roman Catholic order of sisters. Not everyone interviewed has been ordained in the traditional sense and not all have attended seminary. Their roles define who they are.

I also decided not to limit the number of women I interviewed to any one denomination, keeping the focus on the woman and not the denomination. The stories are of clergywomen from the Presbyterian, Methodist, Episcopalian, Baptist, Lutheran, Nazarene, Unitarian Universalist, and United Church of Christ denominations, as well as Roman Catholic sisters, a nondenominational clergywoman and a wedding minister.

The interviews were conducted during 2015 and 2016 and reflect the women's lives at that time. The information contained in each interview came from the women themselves, with no attempt at corroboration from other sources.

In some narratives, the women's ages are listed as context for their stories. Three of the women are young (under forty) because many women enter the clergy as a second career, as do many men.

I found many similarities between the lives of these professional women and my own. Several of the women have mental health credentials comparable to mine. Most were working mothers and more than half have have been married more than once, as have I. So, not surprisingly, I saw myself in some of their experiences.

My heartfelt thanks to all those who agreed to be interviewed, including those I didn't get to in this book, which could have been many chapters longer. And my thanks to those who helped me find such interesting women to interview.

CHAPTER 1
Clergywomen in America

WOMEN HAVE BEEN NOTICEABLY absent from pulpits in America.

They teach Sunday school, prepare communion tables, serve on committees and boards, sing in the choir, play hand bells and organ, wash the windows, iron the altar cloths, tend the flower beds, make coffee and bake cookies for after-service fellowship, water the plants, staff the nursery, and sweep out the building after everyone else has left.

As paid lay workers or volunteers, women have traditionally served as choir director, church secretary, administrative or financial assistant, leader of Christian education, minister of music, and mistress of the manse. In congregations and parishes women deliver meals to the sick, make hospital visits, hand out groceries at food pantries, organize funeral food and receptions, and serve meals to the homeless. They meet in book, Bible study, sisterhood, altar guild, young mothers', and caregivers' groups. When called, they show up, feed, comfort, assist, and support each other.

Women are important in churches and hold many leadership positions. Virtually every major denomination has one or more dedicated women's organization. These include Presbyterian Women, Episcopal Church Women, Women of the Evangelical Lutheran Church in America, United Methodist Women, Woman's Missionary Union of the Southern Baptist Church, United Church of Christ women's website, Hadassah, Catholic Daughters of the Americas, and a host of other church-related women's organizations.

Carol Kuruvilla wrote that women as a group tend to be more religious than men, yet are very underrepresented as pastors. While women are a valued and recognized force in churches in America, ordination of women to the pulpit has been slow. Probably the first significant female religious leader recorded in America was Anne Hutchinson, who encountered serious trouble for her leadership. She was ultimately banished from the Massachusetts Bay Colony and, with her husband, was an early settler of Rhode Island.

Until the last few decades, most congregations rarely saw a woman in the pulpit leading worship on a Sunday morning. Kuruvilla asserts in *The Huffington Post*, "The stained glass ceiling is proving hard to crack—but women are refusing to give up." The 2014 article lists which denominations generally ordain women to the pulpit and which do not (Appendix A).

Some denominations ordain women but then assign them roles as assistant or associate pastor, worship leader or minister of music, director of Christian education, part-time minister, or pastor of small, rural or struggling churches, often in places or circumstances where clergymen do not want to serve. Sometimes women—as do some clergymen—serve more than one church to have a full-time job.

In 1998, Barbara Brown Zikmond and others found that women were more likely than men to finish seminary and then not be ordained. More women than men chose to leave or not enter parish ministry, instead serving in specialized areas such as chaplain in a hospital, hospice, school or prison. At the end of the 20th century, it was still relatively rare to find a woman as a senior pastor in a large church in a mainstream denomination.

However, the number of women clergy had increased significantly in some denominations by the 1990s. Several churches have elected women to the highest office of the denomination in the United States. For example, the Most Reverend Doctor Katharine Jefferts Schori was elected presiding bishop of the Episcopal Church in 2006. Rev. Elizabeth Eaton became the first presiding bishop of the Evangelical Lutheran Church in America in 2013. Rev. Dr. Sharon E. Watkins is general minister and president of the Disciples of Christ, first elected in 2005 and reelected to a second six-year term in 2011. The Presbyterian Church USA has elected nine women to the office of moderator of the General Assembly since 1984.

In 2002, Bishop Sharon Brown Christopher became the first woman to serve as president of the Council of Bishops in the United Methodist Church. Maj. Gen. Lorraine Potter became chief of chaplains for the Air Force in 2001, and Rear Adm. Margaret Grun Kibblen became chief of Navy chaplains in 2014, after being the first chief of Marine Corps chaplains.

It is difficult to determine just how many clergywomen there are in America. Zikmund and fellow researchers found that in fifteen predominantly white Protestant denominations in 1998, twenty-five percent of clergy were women. However, a few denominations had a decreasing number of women ministers, such as the Church of God and the Nazarene Church. A later survey by Christine Smith showed fifteen percent of mainline Protestant denomination ministers were women, compared to seven percent of evangelical/fundamental churches.

According to the Religion News Service in a 2012 National Congregations Study, about eleven percent of individuals surveyed said their head clergyperson was a woman, about the same percentage as 1998. The National Congregations Study in 2012 showed just under three percent female clergy in white conservative, evangelical or fundamentalist congregations; almost sixteen percent women clergy in black Protestant congregations; and almost twenty percent female clergy in white liberal or moderate churches. In 2007, thirty-six percent of seminary students in the U.S. and Canada were women, according to Michael Paulson, citing the Association of Theological Schools in the U.S. and Canada.

Ordination of women in the major denominations is briefly reviewed in Appendix B, along with the notation of which clergywomen in the following chapters represent that denomination. Christine Smith in her 2013 book *The Stained Glass Ceiling* looked at churches employing a female pastor and found the churches were passionate about social justice and had sometimes been founded by a woman. The churches were usually urban or suburban and their current female pastor often was their first clergywoman. The churches sometimes had declining or dying membership and and usually would have preferred hiring a male. She also noted that interim or temporary ministers were often female.

Reasons given across denominations for not selecting a female minister include the assertion that women can't minister to men. Deb Richardson-Moore recounts her strong emotions when a man attending her church, which ministers to the homeless, yelled drunkenly that a woman shouldn't preach and stormed out of the service.

As reasons for not ordaining women, Smith listed Biblical references endorsing the male role in leadership, the time demands of family, traditional values, ageism (often clergywomen are older, having entered the ministry as mid-career changers), and lower expectations of women. A study of American Baptists in 2002 noted that women were more likely to be associate pastors or directors of Christian education, to have lower career mobility, and to begin at a lower starting place than clergymen in their denomination.

In the 1990s, Zikmund and others revealed interesting information about female clergy. However, one must be cautious applying these findings to present-day female clergy.

- Female ministers were more likely to be single than male clergy (thirty-eight percent women versus eight percent men).
- Clergywomen were more likely to have an ordained spouse (forty-two percent women versus eight percent men).
- Fewer female clergy had children under eighteen than male clergy.
- Women were more often in smaller, more isolated parishes and more willing to take lower salaries. This may mean socialization issues outside of the pastorate.
- Among those who were married, fifty percent of women clergy and seventy-five percent of men were in their first marriage.
- Women were perceived as more caring, more sensitive, more nurturing to their congregations, and less interested in congregational politics, power and prestige.
- Women clergy felt less job satisfaction than women in some other professions.
- Salaries were lower for women, even after adjusting for experience and congregational size.

- More women were in non-parish ministry such as hospital, prison or military chaplaincies, social agency (such as hospice) pastoral counselors, or faculty.

Smith says clergywomen bring many skills to their jobs. They multi-task well and become role models for other women. They excel at nurturing and pastoral care. Clergywomen highlight the feminine attributes of God's love as they show their softer side. They usually have strong interpersonal skills. She notes that women entering the ministry need adequate compensation and financial support such as grants and fellowships for their education. Education for churches on the validity of female pastors would help their acceptance, as would recommendations from supportive male and other female clergy to assist in opening doors.

In a study of Nazarene female clergy, Richard Houseal found that younger, smaller congregations are more likely to be accepting of female pastors. Given the aging congregations of many mainstream denominations, this may be a factor in acceptance of clergywomen. A FACT 2010 report documented aging denominations with a large number of congregations with one-third or more congregants aged sixty-five or older. These include American Baptist, Disciples of Christ, Episcopal, Evangelical Lutheran Church of America, Presbyterian, United Church of Christ, and United Methodist Church. They ranged between forty-two percent and sixty-two percent of their congregations falling into the aging category. One might speculate that the trend in many denominations is toward older congregations that may not be as accepting of female clergy, if past research still holds.

The clergywomen's stories in the next several chapters corroborate the findings of some of the research described above.

CHAPTER 2
Pam

PAM WEBB WAS FORTY-SIX years old when she was ordained as an Episcopal priest. Now sixty-seven, she is retired from active ministry and lives in Williamsburg, VA.

When she was baptized at the age of six, Pam put her hands on her hips, looked up at the priest and said, "More water, please!"

Being the youngest and third sibling to be baptized that morning, she felt cheated that the priest had used up almost all the water on her two older brothers. They both got a lot of water and she received only the two or three remaining drops. At the end of the ceremony the priest reminded them they were "sent out to proclaim God's love," so Pam skipped out down the aisle to do just that and had to be retrieved by her parents. She has been spreading God's word one way or another ever since.

Now she finds herself in a new phase of her life after retiring in the fall of 2014. She explains, "I did not retire where I knew anybody … I feel very isolated and I'm not good at isolated. I'm a visitor every Sunday, can't seem to plug in anywhere."

On the path between baptism and retirement, the Episcopal Church has been important in Pam's life as long as she can remember. Her father was a non-practicing Roman Catholic and her mother, a Methodist from a prominent Birmingham, AL, family. Her parents did not want to raise their children in the Roman Catholic tradition, although they were married in the rectory so his parents would recognize the marriage. Her father reportedly said following the wedding, "I'll never set foot in a Catholic church again." He worked for US Steel and the family moved often, living in New Orleans, Fort Worth and Dallas. They moved to Houston when Pam was six years old and affiliated with St. John the Divine, where the children were baptized. Pam considers herself a "cradle Episcopalian."

Pam remembers a significant incident in her young life when she was about four years old. Her mother had colon cancer, was hospitalized for several months, and thought she would die, though she didn't. Her father still took the children to church each Sunday and Pam had outgrown her Sunday shoes. Her mother told her father to take the child to Neiman Marcus and buy another pair of black patent leather Mary Janes. Pam spotted some black velvet, jewel-encrusted children's pumps and begged for those shoes instead.

"Daddy called Mother, who said absolutely not, so he bought me black Mary Janes. I begged. I didn't want Mary Janes. Sunday morning when I got my dress and shoes out to get ready for church, there were the jeweled shoes. I threw my arms around Daddy for getting me the shoes, because I felt so much love and gratitude. Years later I understood this as the metaphor for love of God, of love and gratitude ... the joy of being loved that much."

She laughs when she recalls herself as a child clumping down the aisle, processing with the children's choir in her jeweled shoes. "For my ordination, I was given another pair of shoes like that. I have worn them when I left some parishes." The shoes became an exemplar of "generous love, giving, a sense of gratitude."

Though they moved a lot, Pam's parents always found a church soon after they arrived in a new city. "I loved this, being an extreme extrovert. I have great memories of Sunday school, youth leaders, priests."

The family moved back to Birmingham and Pam vividly remembers the civil rights turmoil of the '60s. She attended St. Luke's, where their youth group leader was fired for marching in a civil rights demonstration. "My father was horrified that he was fired." She attended University of Mississippi—Ole Miss—only a few years after James Meredith had matriculated to racially integrate the university. This turmoil was "part of my formation and observation of the church," she says. "I always knew the church needed to be part of that struggle. I still feel the church needs to be participating in social issues." She says emphatically, "I was raised in the '60s and my church was wrong."

After graduating from college, Pam taught special education in the public schools of Tuscaloosa, then taught and ultimately ran a pre-school at her church at another Episcopal parish for fourteen years. The priest encouraged her to become Christian education director, a job for which she had no training, so she had to learn it all on her own.

A big influence on her career was Dr. Locke Bowman, an Episcopal priest who was a guru of Christian education. Hearing him speak led her to decide to go to seminary some day to study Christian education. "That became my dream."

Her husband said, "You'll never do that." Though she followed him to Virginia for his master's degree, she did not pursue her own at that time. "That dream kept me alive when I didn't have much to go on." They ultimately divorced and Pam talked to her children about her desire to study Christian education. Her daughter was a freshman at Ole Miss, one son was in high school, and the other, in second grade. They encouraged her to go to seminary.

Pam applied to Virginia Seminary, thinking, "They won't take me." Friends told her, "You'll never do it." When she told people she'd been accepted, those friends said, "You'll never leave your house behind"; it had been featured in *Southern Living* magazine. When the For Sale sign was delivered to her house, she pounded it into the ground herself. She took the first offer tendered and sold the house. Her friends said, "You'll fall apart,'" but she recognized a window of opportunity.

"My husband and parents had told me what to wear, what to do, what to say. I was so eager to leave, we finally helped the movers get it done." When they left, friends stood at the end of the driveway, hugging each other and crying while Pam's family jumped in their minivan, waved goodbye and never looked back.

Pam planned to study Christian education and thought she would probably move back to Birmingham after she completed her master's degree. At that time she'd never seen an ordained woman. In 1974, eleven women were ordained as Episcopal priests, an ordination called "irregular" and "invalid" by the church's presiding bishop, but the General Convention in 1976 voted to ordain women and validated the ordination of the original eleven women priests. The past-presiding bishop of the Episcopal Church in America, Katharine Jefferts Schori, was ordained as a priest in 1994, is a pilot and holds a doctorate in oceanography, as well as her doctorate in divinity. The priesthood is the bishop's second career, as it is for Pam and many other clergywomen.

Seminary was a "re-creation, a transformation, the three most positive, most affirming years of my life. I wore bright colors," Pam recalls. "It would never have happened in Birmingham." At seminary, where about one-third of her classmates were female, her fellow seminarians and professors all encouraged her to become a priest.

She went on a retreat to discern spiritual direction and finally said, "OK, God, if this is it, open doors." She applied to her home church and diocese for the endorsement and support required by the seminary but didn't receive it.

She couldn't think of anyone else to ask for endorsement and finally remembered her long-ago priest, the Reverend Frank Vest, who had been her pastor when she lived in Charlotte, NC, many years before. When she mentioned his name to her seminary advisor, he told her, "Did you know he's a bishop now, on our Board of Trustees at Virginia Seminary, and, by the way, meeting on our campus this very week?"

"I said, 'OK, God.'" Pam continues, "I hadn't had contact with him for eleven years and wasn't sure he'd even remember me," though she'd been active in the Charlotte church. He was glad to hear from her when she called, did remember her, and they had breakfast together the next day.

"I told him what I was discerning. He said, 'All you need is a bishop and I'm your bishop.'" He drew her a map on a napkin to show her where his diocese was in south-side Virginia. "He told me, 'You're on your own after this—go find yourself a sponsoring parish.'"

She got a list of parishes and called the rector of a parish in Midlothian, VA. "It all just fell into place. They interviewed me, I preached—I'd never before been allowed even to read in church. The whole decision committee sat on the back pew. When I processed out, they all held up cards with a '10,' Olympic-style." The parish agreed to sponsor her.

She did the discerning process (required by the Episcopal Church) in another parish, received approval from them, and changed her course of study from master of Christian education to master of divinity. She was told she'd never graduate on time after changing her major, but she worked hard and did graduate with her class.

After graduating from seminary, Pam was called to be assistant rector at St. Andrews in Newport News for two years, then rector at Christ Church in Smithfield, VA, for three years, then seven years as rector at St. Johns in Tappahannock, VA. After serving in parishes for twelve years, she returned to Virginia Seminary in Alexandria (for "my dream job, thought I'd retire there") as director of alumni relations. Her first year in that job still stands out as the most enjoyable time in her career.

"I loved the job, thought it would be my life," until a new dean took over and alumni work was de-emphasized. So Pam left. She wonders how her life would have been different had she stayed in her last rector-ship in Tappahannock instead of taking the seminary job.

For the past several years before retirement, she served as interim rector at five different parishes—seven moves in seven years, she notes ruefully, each for about a year. She sees the interim rector's position as "an important ministry. I tried to be an intentional interim rector and prepare the parish for a new priest. Besides, at age sixty, no one was going to call me as a [permanent] rector."

Pam says if she had it to do over again, she would have followed the same path. She muses, "I wonder if my children realize what a risky, brave thing it was [going to seminary], wonder if they're even aware, my never having been an individual [independent] woman before. My brother couldn't take it in. My friends in Birmingham still don't take it in."

Pam is not listed in her home church in Birmingham as someone from there who entered the ministry "and that really hurts my feelings." Even though they didn't sponsor her, she believes she's earned her place on that list. Her parents were dead before she was ordained, but she recalls a dream in which they were looking down approvingly at her.

The best part of her ministerial work has been seeing people grow and become a part of the church. She felt frustration when people were difficult and she didn't ever see change. She speculates if she hadn't become a priest, she probably would have continued in Christian education. "I think I was a church lady."

People react to her differently when she is wearing her clerical collar. When she tells them she's a priest, some say "no way" or "Are you a nun?" While in seminary, she went on a blind date arranged by someone who hadn't told her date what Pam was studying. When he found out, he backed up and said, "I don't do priests!" Another time she was sitting next to a man on an airplane who was coming on to her strongly. He asked what she was reading and when she replied, "The Old Testament," he choked on a peanut and shut up for the rest of the plane ride.

Pam recalls some funny incidents in her work. One time she dressed in the dark and when she looked down later that morning, had on non-matching shoes. At one old church, the air conditioning wasn't keeping the intense heat at bay so she took off her dress before she put on her vestments. When she went to the robing room afterwards, talking with the rector, she unwittingly began taking off her vestments. "I was down to my petticoat with the embarrassed rector saying 'stop, stop.'"

She had some almost-embarrassing moments, such as the Sunday morning she picked up her papers quickly from her office and forgot to include her sermon. She realized her error after the service began and sent an acolyte to run and get it from her office. He brought back the wrong papers so she sent him again and he arrived back with the sermon just in the nick of time.

She also remembers a time when a "pompous, cocky" member of the congregation began his reading to the congregation by announcing "a reading from Paul's letter to the Philippinos." He remained unbelieving when he got back to the pew and his wife told him what he'd said. Pam watched the drama unfold from her perch at the front of the church.

One of her most memorable times in the ministry involved a church renovation. The construction crew removed wallboard in the top of the church and discovered a round window which had been blocked out. Some research revealed it had been a louvered window, probably for ventilation, in the 1800s church building. A family commissioned a stained glass window for the space in honor of their parents, both in a nursing home with Alzheimer's disease. They planned a private family dedication ceremony, bringing both parents to the church in a van from the nursing home.

Pam led the elderly parents around the church, pointing out familiar things with no response from either of them. She recalls they were "totally out of it." She told them, "We'll have a special meal shared with your family today," and the woman lifted her head and said, "Eucharist." Pam said, "We were all floored. Faith is there even if we're not aware of it, of how deeply sacraments have shaped our lives."

If she had her career to do over again, Pam would definitely go into the ministry, in just about the same way. Doing so earlier in her life would not have been possible, partly because there were no women priests in her area at the time. Education was a huge part of it for her. "I used my gifts, my ability to relate to people, to articulate the faith." Her career was most satisfying but also challenging. An established rector sees things grow and receives new people into the parish. "But it's not the same with an interim who just plants the seeds and is then gone by the time they flourish."

The hardest part of her job has been dealing with "wacko people" with difficult personalities: "Different faces, different names but always there. Priests put up with a lot more crap [than in other workplaces] as we model tolerance, a loving attitude, Christian love. It can wear you out because you get some crazies. There are good people everywhere but never enough."

When asked about doubts or spiritual bleakness she may have encountered, Pam says, "I don't think I have actually had a time I felt separated from God or a time of spiritual bleakness. I have had some significant challenges during my ministry but I always felt God's presence during those dark times. Being an extrovert, I have found reaching out to people I respected and trusted to guide and encourage me in those difficult times has been a great resource in overcoming adversities."

With regard to women in the clergy, Pam is sure there were some jobs she didn't get because she was a woman. "You could almost feel when it was a token interview because I was a woman and they were not going to hire me." There is still some differential in pay between women and men in her denomination because of the types of positions women hold, often smaller, more rural churches. There are many women in the Episcopal priesthood "but mostly not the deans of cathedrals, cardinal rectors." Had Pam been male, she believes she "probably would have had opportunities for bigger, more prestigious churches with more resources, opportunities to develop ministries in other places."

Pam has some advice for women—or men—entering the clergy. "First, have a really good support system you can count on in hard times or when you are confused. Know who you can trust, already have relationships developed [before the hard times come]." Second, "Always be willing to risk, try new things to stay fresh, alive." Third, "Discover who you are, work on any identity, faith development issues you need to." Fourth, "Don't be a lone ranger—keep connections in the community, diocese, profession." Fifth, "Beware of high stress—drugs, alcohol. Be constantly vigilant about yourself and others reaching out for help."

Her last recommendation is, "Prepare for retirement—be supportive and sensitive to retirees, reach out to them." She added, "People expect clergy to have it all together all the time. We begin to believe it, too, then feel lost, isolated, when problems occur." These statements reflect Pam's current state of mind as she struggles to redefine herself in retirement. "There are a lot of surprises in retirement," she says. "I'm trying to keep connected, reconnecting. I'm usually extremely positive, energetic, but I could become a slug. Right now I don't initiate."

Her main interests are people, friends and travel. However, she realizes that many of her connections were through her profession. "I realize—that is, I didn't realize—what a huge transition retirement is, a major adjustment in life. I used to be the focus [in church] but now I'm invisible, with no identity. It hit me [recently], how loved I was where I served, respected, people sought me out. Now I have no sense of community, relationship. The phone doesn't ring. I loved the interaction and fulfillment. Now I never look at my calendar."

She adds, "Now that I don't have active ministry, I'm forced to be engaged in scripture. You call on the Spirit to keep spiritual life vibrant and healthy. It's on you when you're not in a church. Much more, I'm the only one accountable. In church, people would know. My spiritual life wouldn't have developed [without ministry]. The challenge now is not to let that atrophy."

At this time of her life, Pam is seeking how to put on her black velvet jeweled shoes and skip out the door into an as-yet-undetermined next phase of her ministry.

CHAPTER 3
Melva

MELVA DRAPER, FIFTY-SIX, IS worship leader / kids' ministry director at Lighthouse Christian Fellowship in Kitty Hawk, NC.

"If God can use Balaam's ass, He can surely use women in ministry. He uses the weak and small," says Melva.

Dressed in a turquoise sleeveless top with lace inserts at the shoulders, white slacks and white leather sandals, Melva is a poised woman who seems secure within herself, no way weak and small. Her well-styled blonde hair with darker highlights makes her appear younger than her mid-fifties. She talks easily, laughs softly, and recites Scripture often and well to punctuate her thoughts.

Melva grew up in a small town in Indiana with two sisters and a brother "who love the Lord and have stayed with church as adults." She says, "I've always known there was a call on my life. When I was small, I'd lie in the grass, look up at the sky, and talk to God. I felt a close relationship with Him. It was just like talking to my dad. Mom told me she and Dad had watched me through the window and they would get tickled. They thought I was talking to myself."

She describes her family of origin as "Godly. I wouldn't use the term 'religious' when describing my parents' faith in God. With them it was about a close personal relationship with God through Jesus Christ." She remembers seeing her father sitting at the table reading the Bible often, especially on Saturday nights when he was preparing for Sunday lessons. Many of her uncles and aunts served in the church, and her father is now preaching in an American Baptist church near where she grew up.

As a child, Melva, after attending revival services with her family, acted on what she had heard in those meetings. She remembers quoting scripture to fellow students when they argued at their four-classroom elementary school in rural Indiana. One time a little boy cried because he was being bullied and not allowed to play king of the mountain with the other boys on the cinder pile behind their small school. Melva marched up to the bully and intoned, "'Get thee behind me, Satan.' He walked away like I was crazy!" She laughs and says she doesn't remember what happened to the little boy who was crying but she does remember that the bully straightened up his act at least for that day.

While she was in high school, Melva began to minister to others intentionally. One of her brother's friends was "making wrong choices, partying, etc." She talked with him and he began to attend church and "came to Christ. He later wrote me a poem ... I still have that poem. That's the joy. The best thing is when someone gets it, grasps hold of the mercy and grace God has for us, allows God to shape them through His word and by His Spirit, and begins to see a transformation that only comes from a contrite heart, bowing down and submitting to our Father. When I see one connecting with God's truth and living totally 'sold out' for Him, that's where I get my joy."

She attended Christian music camp while she was in high

school and was in productions they performed in churches near the camp. She says, "This increased my love and calling for ministry. I had a passion. I remember speaking at a little church, took my guitar and sang songs I wrote. I stuttered and was very shy but God seemed to flow through me when I performed."

While she was in college she belonged to a singing group, Campbellsville College Singers, that was invited to perform at the national convention of the Acteens, a Christian girls' organization, in Kansas City. The singing group was an opening act for popular Christian 1970s and '80s performer and songwriter Andrew Culverwell, a man recognized as influential in the early contemporary Christian music movement. In the style of the time, group members wore loose shirts bloused over skirts with elastic waistbands for easy costume changes, and spike heels. Melva was positioned on a high block and had to climb down to exit the stage. She caught her spike heel in the hem of her skirt and the skirt slid down around her ankles. She was mortified, but managed to exit the stage barely maintaining her composure.

As she burst into tears off-stage, she blindly ran into the arms of Andrew Culverwell, who told her, "Someday this will be a fun memory." More than one person the next day said, "I saw you last night and it wasn't that bad," making her realize just how bad it had been. She laughs and says she remembers the embarrassment but now it has become a fun memory—mostly.

Melva is currently serving in her sixth church. Her path to the present has been convoluted at times. She began her ministry in a church while a student at Campbellsville College in Campbellsville, KY, described on its website as "a private, Christian, liberal arts university located in south central Kentucky." Employed part-time, she served as minister of music but also helped with the youth at that Baptist church. Melva received her undergraduate degree in church recreation, changing her major after having been a music major for three years. She felt called to ministry so decided to combine her interests in music and youth work as she completed her degree.

After her undergraduate work she entered the Southern Baptist Theological Seminary in Louisville, where she received a master of arts in Christian education, graduating when she was twenty-four years old. She served as a youth and music minister in a Baptist church while she was in seminary. She made an important decision for herself about that time, opting not to become an ordained minister.

Baptist ministers are ordained by a particular church after a process of discernment and deliberation, and an American Baptist church was considering Melva for ordination. However, after much thought and prayer, she decided not to take their offer. "Ordained women were not prevalent in ministry at that time, especially as pastors," she explains, although they sometimes held positions as associate pastors or children's ministers. She believed ordination would actually impede her acceptance into the kinds of ministry she wanted to pursue, so she opted to stay un-ordained.

"I made a choice, she says. "Though I was approached to be ordained, I prayed, decided if I was ordained, I may have been limited so I opted not to. All these opportunities opened up after that." She believes that at the time in her denomination, ordination was a plus for a man but could actually limit options for a woman since so many congregations still resisted the idea of a woman leading the church from the pulpit. She notes that although women are becoming more accepted, men still occupy most pastoral leadership roles.

Melva has combined the roles of youth and music ministry.

She says, "Music and youth work go well together. Music is so much a part of youth's lives—'YouTube,' 'America's Got Talent.' Many of them idolize musicians. A youth leader who is also a musician can use those skills to connect to youth and open many doors for them to open up to you." Melva plays piano and sings, skills that allow her to be a worship leader.

After she graduated from seminary, two churches offered her jobs. During the interview process, she thought, "Both said, 'God led us to you,' so how do I know where God wants me to be?" One was a large, prestigious church within three hours of her home where she would have had three other ministers working under her supervision, with about eight hundred people attending weekly services. "It sounded so neat." The other was farther away, a smaller Baptist church on the Outer Banks of North Carolina with about two hundred fifty active members, "nothing prestigious about the position, felt home-grown."

She thought, "'Lord, how do I know?' I just trusted God, came to the smaller church where I could be more of a hands-on person." She worked there for five years in youth and music ministry.

Her life changed after she moved to the small coastal North Carolina town. "Everyone was a native, skeptical of outsiders. They didn't want change. I was single at that time, fourteen hours from home and my close family. They were nice folks and the pastor and his family supported me, but I felt like an outsider." Now, about thirty years later, she feels like a native herself in that same small town. She remembers when there was just one stoplight on the beach, a place now replete with traffic and traffic signals.

However, a new pastor came to the church and Melva had "a sad leaving. I didn't handle it well, at my [young] age. But that's how we learn." The new pastor and she "didn't see eye to eye about the music. He feared I was too charismatic." She laughs and says, "I don't fit in a mold. I'm not as charismatic as he thought, but not as Baptist as some think, either."

Melva recalls about herself, "Some bitterness took hold." She left the ministry and asked her father, "Daddy, can I come home?" receiving the answer of "Sure." However, someone in her former church offered her a job and she became a real estate appraiser for Dare County, NC. She stayed because "I felt I belonged here." However, she said she had to "take one more trip around Mt. Sinai until I got it," referring to the Biblical story of Moses wandering for seven years around Mt. Sinai, never getting to go to the Promised Land with his people. "It was my wilderness experience."

Although not employed as a minister, she began working with other single people who started Christian Singles United. The group enrolled fifty or sixty members and became an important support group for her.

For five years she was a tax appraiser. She got to work alone on projects, something she'd never done as a minister, and "was done when I went home. My private life was no longer on show." She had had little dating life while she worked in the church—"No one wanted to date the church lady. I had one date the whole time I was at the church and it was not good. He talked down about country mentality of the people in the church and said he would never pursue a relationship with anyone under his level of education." Melva thinks life education is more valuable than formal schooling.

She laughs, "I ended up marrying a garbage collector." Her husband of sixteen years, Billy, was head of a city sanitation department before he retired. She says, "I always said I will never marry a divorced person, but never say never!" She married Billy and inherited four stepchildren, who lived with them for a while.

"When you marry a man with children and an ex-wife, it is a package deal," she says. "Not just the children, but the children's mother, too. You must respect and honor her. You may not agree with her, but those children are hers. She bore them into this world. It's kind of like a marriage, 'till death do us part.' God has done a work in both of us. It's a very humbling experience."

She learned from her work experience in the secular world. "I felt like I didn't belong. It was gossipy, and I got a taste of what the world was like. I didn't fit in well. God used it as a dose of reality. A minister can live in a bubble. It helped me to understand culture. I had to try to *live* in it but not *be* in it." She says, "We as ministers who work in our world have protection [through trust in God] but it's so easy to fall. It's a harder crash because people put you on a pedestal. But you're flesh, not a little Christ. That's the hardest thing, the pedestal. Sometimes you put yourself there."

While she was still a tax appraiser, another Baptist church on the Outer Banks invited her to come and sing at a women's conference. Little did she know that she was auditioning for a job. A week later she received a phone call asking her to be their minister of music, a job she held and loved for several years. Then the church split and she found herself enveloped in the resulting bitterness. She stayed for a few months but left to find different employment. She remembers, "I didn't want to be a part of the bitterness. I felt that people were trying to drag me to one side or the other. This made it very difficult to lead worship there."

Currently Melva is employed as worship leader / kids' ministry director at Lighthouse Christian Fellowship in Kitty Hawk, where she has served for twelve years. She is in a part-time position because twelve years ago she adopted a child with special needs. She describes him as a delightful, gifted young man but the demands of parenting make part-time work a better option for her at present. She also teaches piano and voice lessons part-time. She tells her students, "Stick to it and practice." She says, "It's the same thing with God. Stick to it, run the race, see your life changed and live to the fullest that God has for you."

As a worship leader, she directs the parts of the church service that rely on music, both performing and leading others to participate in worship. The Lighthouse is a non-denominational church and she and husband Billy lead worship together: "He is an awesome musician, plays piano and guitar. I believe that God has put us together to lead worship."

Although Melva has occasionally preached in other churches, she no longer does so because she doesn't want to be a "stumbling block" as some might view her in the pulpit. However, she has led adult Bible studies at her pastor's request. She says her heart is in leading worship and music ministry.

"I don't think I ever sought it. It sought me. God seeks one, not always a Damascus Road experience [referring to the apostle Paul's conversion]." She respects the view of church members who cite scriptural references refusing women roles of authority in the family or the church. "I want God to use me. It's not about me. I don't need a title to serve Him."

Melva describes herself in this way: "I am an open book. I wear my feelings on my sleeve, I hope not in a bad way. This is good for a minister. You need to relate, understand emotion, people who are hurting. If you can't feel and express that, you can't counsel others. We have to control how we express ourselves—that comes with maturity. We must cry with those who need it."

She confides that she herself has dealt with depression and at times felt like a failure because she had to take an anti-depressant. She now believes that God heals through medicines and we must end the stigma of mental illness. She used the medicine for five years before she weaned herself off and helps others understand that "God gave you that medicine if you need it." She says, "This is a big ministry for me, not through the church, but people whom God puts along my path."

God has helped her through her own medical issues. She remembers a time when she was recovering from surgery, wandering around her house trying to walk off the pain. A voice told her to practice thankfulness. Because she was in so much pain, she didn't think she could do that. But she glanced around her kitchen until she spotted her toaster and begrudgingly thanked God for her toaster. It was the beginning of trying to think of something she was thankful for, though she didn't feel it. She went on to enumerate other things in her home for which she was thankful and eventually began to focus on God's goodness and great love.

"God's presence fell upon me and this one simple practice of gratefulness in a time of great pain became one of the sweetest encounters with my beloved Father. Before I knew it, I had been praising and worshipping God for more than two hours, forgetting about myself." She says, "We don't practice gratefulness enough. We need to practice gratefulness. Sometimes I just think of that toaster."

If a woman asked her advice about going into the ministry, she would say, "Do not go into it lightly. You probably won't get paid for your hours. Don't go into it for the money. That's why it's a calling, not an occupational choice." Melva laments that many people do not understand her job, what she does all day.

"There's little money and it's very emotionally draining,

even spiritually draining. Everything is preparation for something. If you're not careful, you will lose your own time with God. You have to spend time alone with God. Set a time and stick with it. That can sometimes be a struggle, time interrupted. Rely on God's strength." She is aware that she has sometimes been paid less than the man who had previously held the position. She says, "I can't dwell on that. Times have changed for the better."

A frustration of her job is scheduling volunteers, though a large portion of the adults volunteer for something in her current church. Keeping people involved can be challenging. She says, "Commitment is hard to come by with volunteers due to their schedules. I am grateful to all volunteers who want to serve. Everyone has a place in God's family."

When asked about her approach to sharing the gospel, she says, "Sometimes people get so zealous, it's like they are pushing it in people's faces. In college, there were a few male students who carried big black Bibles and preached hellfire and brimstone. We called them the Bible-beaters Association in seminary. They want to preach to you and beat you over your head with it. Sometimes gentleness and kindness speak of Christ better."

Handling friendships within the church can be difficult. "It can be hard to find your own place in a church when you're a minister. It can be lonely. Some people are in awe and don't tend to be friendly. Others want to buddy up, seems like they think they're almost higher in church if they're closer to the minister." She says early on she made a lot of mistakes, including confiding in someone when she shouldn't have.

"Sometimes you have to find that outside support group, outside of your own church. Women need to share. In my current church family, this has not been as much of a problem. We are close-knit, bearing one another's burdens. I have found a church family I can be real with. That is not as common as you might think. I thank God for them."

Living in a resort area offers special opportunities for ministry. "Worship on the beach, Jesus-style," invites the website of SAIL Ministries at the Outer Banks. The group offers an Easter passion play on the sand dunes at Jockey's Ridge in Kill Devil Hills, and Melva wrote the first script for that event. She says, "It was hard to let go of that ministry." She, along with Agnes Blanchard and Angela Noffsinger, joined Greg Wise in beginning SAIL, now headed up by Wise and his wife, Cindy. Melva says, "I stepped down from that ministry a couple of years later when I was called to a full-time position at Kitty Hawk Baptist Church."

Melva sees a pattern developing over her years of service. Each church has been smaller than the last. She says, "Success is defined in the world as getting a bigger and better position in a bigger organization with more pay and benefits. Not so in working for the Lord. I enjoy working in smaller churches. There is a tighter-knit sense of family closeness. Everyone is needed in the body of Christ." However, in the summer in a resort community, people work long hours and churches need to "plug people in as they come in, keep the family mentality as we grow, embody Christ in our lives."

She notes that when the church is smaller, there are fewer people to do the work. "It seems that in my experience in most larger churches and some small ones, twenty percent of the people do eighty percent of the work." However, in her church now, she says about eighty percent of the people "are plugged into a position of service. I believe that we can get so large that people feel they are not needed so they can get complacent. God has a purpose for everyone in His church."

She believes the goal is to have a family atmosphere.

"Everyone should be truly concerned with each other's burdens and delight in their joys. It's important to plug people in as they come in, let them know they are a vital member of the church, keep the family mentality as we grow and not let people feel disconnected."

Melva resists being pigeon-holed in her work. She says, "What is true worship? Some raise their hands, some sing choruses, some clap their hands. I want it to be worship, an experience. I'm not a good Baptist nor a good charismatic. I just want all that God has for me, whatever that is." Melva says both are great as long as it is true worship "from the heart, born out of a relationship with God. Style doesn't matter. I believe, don't throw out the traditional if it's good. Where's the Doxology these days?"

She sums up her attitude toward ministry with, "I think the Holy Spirit is gentle. Authority is not an issue. We must gently serve. Philistines 4:4 says, 'Rejoice in the Lord. Let gentleness be evident to all. The Lord is near.'" Though she says she falls short more times than she'd like to admit, Melva strives to live this belief in all aspects of her life.

*Error: Should be Philippians 4:4

CHAPTER 4
Michele and Monique

MICHELE VAN VOORST, NINETY-THREE, and Monique Dietz, eighty-one, are members of the Ladies of Bethany order of the Roman Catholic Church. They live in Pittsburgh, PA, after emigrating to America from the Netherlands about fifty years ago, and are retired from their jobs but very active volunteers in their city.

"We hid under the kitchen table with bullets whizzing by," Monique recalls of World War II, though she says of that daunting experience, "It's peanuts compared to the destruction of wars today." The Netherlands had declared neutrality, but the German army invaded and occupied the country anyway. Both Monique and Michele remember the war in the 1940s in the Netherlands very clearly and see that time as influential in their becoming nuns.

Both women belong to the Ladies of Bethany, founded in the Netherlands in 1919. They were not acquainted with each other before entering the order, though they hailed from the same city—The Hague—the same neighborhood and the same parish. They came to America in the 1960s as emissaries of the Ladies. The order is diminished now, as are many other religious communities. Always small, never more than one hundred twenty sisters, their ranks have now shrunk to twenty-five.

Michele wears short hair, clothing a few years shy of fashionable, sensible shoes and a ready smile. A small brooch of colorful stones anchors her sweater. In her nineties, fluent and coherent, she defies age stereotypes. "I was a child of the war," she says. She graduated from high school in 1940 and attended secretarial school, about which she says, "It was better than nothing." When her hopes for a university education were dashed by the outbreak of World War II, her thirst for learning was met instead when she entered the Ladies of Bethany in 1945. There she pursued ecumenical studies including philosophy, Bible studies, theology and human nature in an ecumenical setting—pastoral care in general.

World War II was a significant part of her life. Michele remembers the German army invading Holland. Her family, as was Monique's, was forced to evacuate from the Hague due to German occupation of their neighborhood.

Her father was a general, second in command of the Dutch army, who spent five years as a prisoner of war under the Nazi regime. "He could have evaded prison by promising not to undertake any action against the German occupiers during the war, but he would not do that because he had sworn allegiance to the Queen," Michele explains. She recalls the populace being very angry with Germans because they imposed restrictions. "The Germans took a lot of stuff. Then came the bombs and we were scared." When her family was evacuated from the Hague, they lived with an aunt while her father was imprisoned.

Michele's family was very religious. "I already had the desire to become a nun, before the war." Her family included two boys and seven girls, three of whom joined the Ladies of Bethany. The two boys joined the Jesuits. Other family members were also in the Ladies of Bethany, including an aunt and a cousin.

The Netherlands was about forty percent Catholic and forty percent Protestant during World War II, with many Jewish people also. Relationships between Catholics and Protestants evolved as people of faith struggled with the German occupation. Many Dutch people harbored Jewish families, such as Anne Frank described in her diary set in Amsterdam, but many other Jews were transported to concentration camps. A hero of the time was the Roman Catholic Archbishop Johannes de Jong, later Cardinal de Jong. He was considered one of the major leaders against the Nazi occupation. Michele says people in prisons came together regardless of church heritage and prayed, contributing to the ecumenical attitude of the country.

The charism—the spiritual orientation or mission of the Ladies of Bethany—is ecumenical work within the community at large. When the community was about forty years old, the Ladies decided to become more worldwide in influence. The order expanded to Germany, Austria, Spain and the United States. Having a more worldwide focus gave the Ladies more vocational opportunities.

American Bishop John Wright—later Cardinal Wright—welcomed the sisters from the Netherlands to Pittsburgh. "He seemed to understand our ideas for outreach. We are a group of women concerned about people, whatever they are going through. We want to help people to become not Catholic but human people." Two sisters of the order came initially and eventually there were six Ladies of Bethany working in the Pittsburgh area, with Michele the sixth to arrive.

In a letter to the Church of Pittsburgh in 1993, the late Jacinta van Winkel, a member of the order and a professor at Carlow

College, wrote of the Bishop, "He liked our concern for the people without faith, our desire to go out and find people where they were, in the workplace, the home or on the street. He also encouraged our desire to seek cooperation with Christians of other denominations."

Michele says, "Bishop Wright wanted to bring the church into the kitchen," to personalize the church and its work where people lived, not just in the church buildings.

Michele and the other Ladies do not wear habits, nor are they called "sister." Though children of the war, they matured as women fulfilling the Vatican II awakening of the early '60s with emphasis on ecumenical work. Michele says, "We were on the forefront of change," fulfilling the charism of the Ladies of Bethany to participate in the daily life of large cities with much poverty. She remembers with a laugh, "It was difficult for the convent on the other side [across the bridge in Pittsburgh] to see us with no habit. They were jealous!"

The Ladies of Bethany moved into a farmhouse on the outskirts of a housing development called North View Heights. They called it The Vineyard. As activities outgrew the limited space, the Diocese of Pittsburgh built an adjacent activities center. Programs included religious education for children and teens, clubs, music, plays, a library, summer day camps and more. Van Winkel says in her 1993 letter, "However, the assassination of Dr. Martin Luther King in 1968 and the disturbances that followed gradually changed the climate. We were advised that it was best to turn over the center, the house, and the programs to citizens of the community itself."

The Ladies of Bethany left the Vineyard in the '70s after running it for nine years. The center was initially about sixty percent white families, forty percent black, but it became ninety-nine percent black and the sisters felt others could run it better. The Vineyard was sponsored by the diocese but staffed by white Dutch women, who believed there should be black leadership. The center transitioned to secular black leadership, but the new bishop kept the church's commitment to the Vineyard even after the Ladies left.

The six Ladies of Bethany also established The Ark and The Dove, an ecumenical retreat center in a lovely rural setting in the North Hills of Pittsburgh. Later Michele joined the East End Cooperative ministry begun by Presbyterians and Catholics to minister to homebound elderly. No official services existed, "So I began the ministry, with all my education," she says, laughing.

She became involved with various agencies and more churches as they established services for teenagers and children, as well as continuing to minister to the homebound elderly. "Groups came together, it grew and became bigger and bigger, very important time for that area." She worked there for twenty-seven years, "always for the homebound elderly." Vista, AmeriCorps, and other religious groups became involved, with eventually forty-five Christian churches representing fifteen denominations, plus synagogues and temples. They brought Meals on Wheels to the community and founded a food pantry and a soup kitchen. Michele says, "We would talk to people and see their needs."

In 2013, the East End Cooperative Ministry was able to consolidate all its ministries in one newly built center. Michele retired in 2000 but volunteers at the center, and at the age of ninety-three says, "I still like what I do."

Asked if she would enter the sisterhood of the Ladies of Bethany again, Michele replies without hesitation that she would, but do it differently. "I would hope to do it better; you always see your mistakes, shortcomings. I would have liked more education, how to deal with people better." She continues, "I'd listen more to what God has to say to me. Often we don't know what God's saying. With a second chance, I would do it better."

Michele would not have wanted to be a priest if she had had the opportunity. "I would have to do sermons and I couldn't do it." She would have been a priest who worked in the community, not in the pulpit. "Proclamation of Gospel is important but I'm happy not to be a priest. I'm satisfied to be with people, to see what their needs are. If I help them become a more full-fledged person, that makes me happy."

She explains that material goods are not important to her. "Not that I have it all, just to be there and share what I may have, to listen. I can be enriched by poor people. It makes me happy to have people that inspire me." She adds with a laugh, referring to the interview for this book, that she was initially unsure of doing the interview but, "Now I think it makes me happy."

Michele's advice to women who may want to live in a religious community is to decide, "Am I really inspired by the work, what these women are doing, would I like to commit myself? Try to discern if God is calling them to that community."

Or, in Michele's words, "Go try it and pray."

Monique sports a halo of short, fluffy white hair and converses animatedly as she describes her years of work. Her energy belies her age; one would never guess she is in her early eighties. She has been a member of the Ladies of Bethany for sixty years, entering the order in 1956. By then she had earned a master of science degree in chemistry, influenced by a high school chemistry teacher, and planned to become a teacher or do research. She did not feel that she had a vocation for religious life so she pursued chemistry. "I figured I should at least have a major so I could have a job," if she eventually decided to enter the convent and later it didn't work out.

She chose a science major even though she was more interested in literature and other humanities. But the chemistry major ... "It didn't really fit me." She was acquainted with the Ladies of Bethany because they had provided her religious education when she was in high school. When she was in her late teens, she had known several young people who died. "That set me thinking, what to do with my life, what or whom in my life I could trust."

This introspection led her back to the Ladies of Bethany. "They seemed to see something in me," although the relationship didn't initially feel like a vocation. Within her religious community, she studied theology and pastoral care. She also has a master's in social work from the University of Pittsburgh and a doctorate in ministry from Notre Dame.

She downplays the value of her degrees: "I consider what I learned in school not as important as what I learned in life but I had to get the paper" to be able to get jobs and have credibility in the workplace. The Ladies of Bethany have a tradition of not living in a convent and they support themselves through paid work so her degrees were very valuable when the Ladies no longer worked in the community centers they had founded and had to find jobs in the world at large.

Even though a decade younger, Monique's war memories parallel Michele's. Her family, evacuated from the Hague in 1943, went to live in a very rural area. Everyone there was a farmer—except for a doctor, the mayor, a minister, and Monique's father, a lawyer. She felt her family was not very well accepted in the community, literally having to elbow their way into church pews which already had a well-established seating pattern. "People had their own places. We had to fit in all the time."

An important event occurred for Monique while they were living in the country. Her family, which she describes as very religious, attended a New Year's Eve service at church. Everyone had been baking doughnuts for the holiday and the church smelled delicious from the baking odor people carried in with them. Seventy years later, she says, "I can still smell it." The priest preached that life changed rather than being taken away when people died, and that idea had a big impact on the young Monique.

In 1963 Monique came to America to join other Ladies of Bethany doing community service work. She was the fifth of six nuns who came to Pittsburgh to work in a poor urban area.

Newly built housing projects sheltered the poor in Pittsburgh at that time. The children living there needed religious education and the Ladies were asked to respond to that need. Thus The Vineyard, a community center providing religious education and social services, was founded. When they outgrew the building, the basement and the attic of the former farmhouse, the Diocese built a new center and the women recruited volunteers from colleges and high schools to help staff it. They were serving not only Catholics but others as well. "We were even more concerned about those who hadn't met Christ." The Ladies staffed the center from 1963 to 1971.

When the Ladies developed The Ark and The Dove, their emphasis was helping people to grow ecumenically. Monique remembers during the renovation daily traversing the sixteen miles separating the the Vineyard and the new center and trying to keep everything running smoothly.

In 1971, the six Ladies of Bethany all found new ministries. Some were already at The Ark and The Dove while others went elsewhere and had to find a way to earn a living. This sisterhood is different from others in the Catholic church in not having as specific a mission as teaching or nursing orders do. They are committed to improving community life among the poor in various ways.

According to an April 2015 article in the Pittsburgh Catholic newsletter, based on a 1993 letter by Jacinta van Winkel to the church, the then five remaining Ladies of Bethany included a retired professor, a psychologist, a pastoral minister, a worker at an ecological center and a community volunteer. To date, three remain in the United States; two of them are the interviewees in this chapter and one serves a college population in Chicago. The other two of the remaining five nuns returned to the Netherlands in recent years due to physical problems related to advancing age.

Monique earned her master's degree in social work in 1973. According to van Winkel's 1993 letter, "Monique worked for creative developments in ministries to the elderly, allowing them as much as possible to stay in the neighborhood where they had lived most of their lives." Monique became director of the Vintage Senior Center co-sponsored by the East End Cooperative ministry. She resigned after two years, the only time she ever resigned from anything, saying with amusement, "In religious life you never said no. I never figured out you could say no!"

She then worked at a creative aging program. She says, "Old people are being shelved when they need to keep being creative." She assumed leadership roles in organizations dedicated to improving life for seniors. She convinced the diocese to give permission to convert vacant small houses that formerly sheltered nuns to apartment housing for older adults. She developed a continuum of care that included senior housing and health care.

After working two years internationally for the Ladies of Bethany community, in 1990 Monique became a hospital chaplain in a secular hospital, where she served for twenty years. It was not the job she would have chosen. She'd been trained in group work and community organization in social work but there was no money at that time for ministries in those fields.

"Diocesan priorities tried to eliminate this ministry five times," Monique says with a laugh—among other reasons, "because I was a woman running a chaplaincy. Priests who needed to assist me were not happy [with a woman leader], to say the least. I told them, what I do in the hospital, my business; what you do in the church, your business." She finally was let go from that job by the hospital's decision, recalling, "There comes a time when you can't do a job anymore."

Then she began doing peace and justice work at the Thomas Merton Center in Pittsburgh. She was living part of the Ladies of Bethany Community faith statement: "As members of Bethany we are committed to promoting the dignity of women and men, and justice and peace in human societies."

Monique would not have wanted to be an ordained priest, had that path been open to her. "The church would have to change first. I'm a 'congregational' person, not 'hierarchical.'" She has been satisfied with her work. "I was a pioneer, doing new ministries, all new things."

She believes she has been "much enriched, to come from Europe to a country struggling with racism." She says she has been grateful to be a part of that era and once heard someone say, "She's a real [black] sistah!" She adds, "I was part of ministries with always something new, exciting, enriching." She wonders, "Was there a thread, stepping stones to hospital chaplaincy?" and concludes, "The older I get, the less I know!"

She says she isn't sure she'd enter the community again, adding somewhat wistfully, "I would like to have had a family, children." But she quickly says that she wouldn't want to have missed doing the work she's done.

Monique sees people not joining religious life in the Western Hemisphere as they did in the past. "People are searching for where we're going; where we've been isn't it." She believes, "We are now in 'middle space,' not knowing about the future." Most religious communities are diminishing, dying. Others may assume a different model in the future, such as those described by Nathan Schneider in a 2015 article, "New Monasticisms."

Monique invites those interested in a religious vocation to "join us in the search, join us in middle space trying to discern the future." She ruefully adds that the future may include a lot of older sisters to care for, no religiously staffed schools or hospitals, financial problems, and large empty properties.

The joy and love these two aging nuns exude is clearly transforming for the people they have touched in Pittsburgh and around the world.

CHAPTER 5
Cathie

CATHIE BRAMAN, SIXTY-EIGHT, IS an ordained minister of the United Church of Christ (UCC). She lives in Fredericksburg, VA, and operates a business called Animal Rites.

Cathie drives a little red Suzuki with the license plate PETREV. A diminutive woman whose smile and presence light up a room, she is an ordained minister of the United Church of Christ. These days she has redirected her efforts from serving as clergy in a traditional religious setting to ministering to those grieving loss of their pets.

Married to Walter, a clergyman of the Unitarian Universalist Fellowship, Cathie has two adult children and two grandchildren. She was ordained at the age of fifty and reflects, "I wish I'd been able to do ministry from an early age, gone to seminary right out of college instead of wasting my time … never found anything that fit me before I went into the ministry."

Her childhood in the small town of Whitman, MA, centered around her family, school, and her church. Cathie recalls her school and church life as being entwined, with little else to do in the smallest town in Massachusetts, the home of Toll House cookies. Her friends at church were also her friends at school.

Church services every Sunday, vacation Bible school every summer, and various other events at the church helped shape her life. At that time junior high school students were dismissed early once a week to attend religious instruction at their own churches. Cathie recalls walking down the street with her best friend, stopping at the local bank to see what freebies might be on offer—a comb, a ruler she still has—then continuing on to her UCC church while her friend veered off to the Catholic church.

Cathie and her parents formed a close-knit family. Her dad worked for Massachusetts Electric for forty-six years and her mother went to work as a school secretary when Cathie was a teenager. She grew up in one of the oldest houses in town, probably dating to the 1740s, and says, "I still miss that house."

She reflects, "Thank God we had that church" as a part of her life. She worries that teenagers today don't have that kind of anchor. "Kids can't sit still anymore, iPads, iPhones, all the rest ... I don't envy youth group leaders these days. Kids need to slow down!" Then she ruefully comments how busy her own life is lately and thinks maybe she should take her own advice.

Pets are an important part of Cathie's life. Her first pet was a cat when she was little, but Cathie had asthma so the cat had to go. However, she explains with a laugh, the cat went to a farm with cows where they made ice cream, so she believes it had a happy life. This first experience with a pet was far from her last and may have helped inspire the Pet Reverend of today.

The next pet appeared after her husband took a job in Maine, where they lived in an apartment above the sanctuary. A little black cat followed Walter home and up the stairs one day. The pregnant Cathie fell in love with the little cat, which had feline leukemia and died only a few months later. She disregarded her physician's advice to wait awhile before acquiring another cat, went to the humane society, and adopted one. Then they visited someone with a new litter of kittens and got two more. Then another cat showed up in the yard, they fed it … a fourth cat. By the time they left Maine, they had four cats—Snowball, Beauty, Vicki, and Sam—along with a rabbit, Thumper, and a dog, PC.

The rabbit died in Maine but the rest of the menagerie accompanied them to Walter's new assignment in Kingston, MA. Then on one visit home from college, Cathie's daughter brought home an abandoned cat … Fred. Nine years later when they moved to Virginia, the cats Vicki, Fred and Sam, and the dog PC accompanied them. Cathie and Walter now live with an eighteen-year-old dog, Phoebe, five indoor cats and one that lives outside.

During a pre-candidating sermon for Walter at a prospective new church, Cathie began talking at coffee hour to a woman, a stranger there. The woman encouraged her to enter the ministry, saying, "You should definitely do it, Cathie." Others at that coffee hour either did not see or later did not remember the woman. Cathie said she also saw the mysterious stranger on one other occasion at a meeting and to this day calls it "my angel experience."

Following the encouragement of the "angel," Cathie contacted the Bangor (ME) Theological Seminary to request enrollment information. She had a bachelor of arts in psychology and sociology from Bridgewater State University, so was ready for a graduate program. Out of the blue she received a call from Andover Newton Theological School in Newton, MA, offering her a chance to apply to the seminary. She was admitted without ever formally applying and feels it was "meant to be."

When she announced she'd be attending seminary, she remembers her mother saying, "Oh, brother! We wanted her to go to Katy Gibbs [secretarial school] but she wasn't interested."

Cathie already had a busy life when she matriculated at Andover Newton. She had worked as a secretary and computer specialist in her pre-seminary years. Her daughter was a teenager and her son, three years old. Her husband was a minister with a somewhat flexible schedule and she credits him and her parents for helping with child care so she could attend seminary.

Cathie did not have a discerning moment about becoming a minister: "It was just there … didn't slap me in the face. I just knew this was what I should do." The invitation from Andover Newton when she hadn't even applied reinforced her belief that her life was headed where she was called. The seminary is a UCC-American Baptist establishment that historically counts abolitionists and other liberal thinkers among its graduates.

In seminary Cathie and four other women formed a support group that has lasted through the years. Most of the women are still in touch with each other. She had several influential women professors at the seminary, including a former Roman Catholic nun who had converted to the UCC church. About half the students in her class were women; Cathie says she was in the forefront of the wave of women seeking preparation for a second career in the church.

She recalls her fieldwork as a crucial seminary experience when she was assigned to the church she'd grown up in but hadn't attended for the previous twenty-five years. She speculates that wouldn't have been a good placement immediately after her membership but many years later gave her good perspective on her training.

She found a lifelong influence in the pastor there, "a fantastic mentor." Cathie describes him as a person who "had ADHD to the Nth degree," always out with people in the community, not necessarily members of his church. He was "very, very centered, a real pastor" who would "stay out until one a.m. with someone under a bridge if necessary." She says he had "way too many books!" Perhaps she learned from him how to fashion a person-centered ministry based on theological writing.

Cathie's first pastorate was as interim minister at a UCC church in Rockland, MA, where she then became the pastor and served almost five years. The United Church of Christ was formed from the Congregational, Christian, Evangelical, and Reformed traditions, resulting in the establishment of the UCC in 1957. The national website, www.ucc.org, describes the church as supporting a "just and sustainable world" seeking to "Do justice, seek peace, and help to change the world." One section of the website is titled "Advocate for Justice" and lists alternatives for social action.

She resigned when her husband took a job some distance away but actually stayed one year longer than she'd intended, at the church's request. The church sold the parsonage and realized enough money to rent her an apartment for her additional year. Unfortunately, she recalls, that real estate decision caused a split in the church so she wonders if, for the good of the church, she perhaps should have left a year earlier, as she'd originally planned.

The sixteen hours a week she contracted for at the Rockland church turned into much more time commitment. Cathie remembers, "I loved being out of the church, out in the community," describing the Rockland clergy as a very collegial group who did a lot of planning for community work together. For example, the Roman Catholic priest would invite Protestant ministers to preach in his church. She enjoyed working with other ministers for the good of all, to a degree unusual in a community. "The people ... I loved working with the people," says Cathie of that time.

The most difficult part of her job, both in Rockland and elsewhere, has been "people's personalities," universal difficulties that seem to exist for everyone everywhere, regardless of profession or location. She recalls that "a couple of women [in Rockland] made it very difficult for me to stay" during the additional unplanned year she spent there as pastor.

In 2003 Cathie became the founding pastor of the Fredericksburg Congregational Church, UCC, in Fredericksburg, VA, after conversations with other like-minded Christians in the community. The denominational hierarchy was not initially supportive because the financial base wasn't what the leaders considered sufficient. However, the church was born, meeting in rented space, including a coffee shop in a shopping center. There were usually twenty to thirty people at a service and the congregation has now been fully recognized by the UCC organization. She enjoyed the ministry, but began to feel some distance from her congregation when she announced her decision to leave the part-time position as minister due to increasing time commitments in other areas of her life.

Women have been well-accepted as ministers in the UCC. Cathie says when she graduated from seminary, there were far fewer women pastors than there are now. When she received her first call to a church, the general expectation was that pastors would be men, but she herself has never felt any personal discrimination because of her gender. Cathie speculates that any existing pay discrepancies between male and female clergy in the UCC may result from where women serve, as each congregation invites its own pastor and sets the salary. Often women serve in smaller, more rural isolated parishes, regardless of the denomination, providing less financial compensation.

During the course of her ministry, Cathie became somewhat disillusioned with the bureaucracy of her denomination. For example, some leaders disagreed with her about establishing the Fredericksburg church, an action that was later validated. Cathie tells about a time she and some of her congregation attended a meeting at a large UCC church with a broken elevator. Her group included a woman unable to walk up and down steps, required for participation in the day's activities. People at the host church were not helpful in solving the problem, so the men from her congregation helped the disabled woman up and down the steps.

Cathie relates, "Most of us felt we hadn't been treated well." At home she preached a sermon on the incident "from my vantage point, what I saw." The sermon was very well-received by Cathie's congregation and she sent a copy to a woman in the UCC hierarchy. The woman became furious and "came calling" to castigate Cathie, as well as mailing the sermon to others in the church administration. Cathie remembers, "I was shunned … it hurt," after she had spoken from "what we all felt that day." It was a disillusioning experience in church bureaucracy for Cathie.

Cathie believes many people now find "spirituality outside the church," more than when she first became a minister. It's more difficult these days to get people to attend church, she thinks, and states her philosophy, "If somebody leaves the church, let them leave." The minister often doesn't know why the person disappears, she speculates, but the more involved someone is in the church, the more chance they can be hurt by someone else's words or disapproval, Cathie speculates. Then a person may withdraw over embarrassment at being hurt. Sometimes a minister finds out years later why someone departed, as Cathie hopes will happen with a former congregant who has recently resumed contact with her through Facebook.

Being half of a clergy couple has made Cathie a better minister, she believes. "Walter is very Biblically literate. We discuss ideas and it has enhanced my ministry by challenging what I know and think." Even though Cathie no longer pastors a church and Walter is about to be declared pastor emeritus in his church (Unitarian), they still debate theological issues, apparently with great zest. She reflects that she would not now be in the life she enjoys in Virginia, had they not moved there with Walter's job, something she calls a "God-cident," an incident arranged by God.

Cathie says the greatest joys of being a minister for her were "being in the life process, marriage, birth, etc.," and "I loved preaching, putting a sermon together with a table full of books, Bible, commentaries." Her face lights up as she recounts sermon construction and one can envision the small woman dwarfed by a table piled with books and papers.

She says the best moment of her work so far was participating in a community coalition to prepare for the two-hundred-twenty-fifth anniversary of Thomas Jefferson signing the Religious Freedom Act, a historic event that occurred in Fredericksburg. She says wistfully, "Wish we could do it again!" The Mary Washington University Dodd Auditorium hosted representatives from area faiths—temples, mosques, and churches. Native Americans attended early discussions on the celebration and all but one of the mainline Protestant denominations in town participated. Participants each presented a three-minute summary of their faith/church/denomination and it was a harmonious event.

Cathie's most embarrassing moment in the church occurred because she did not take her mentor's advice when he told her, "Never say the Lord's Prayer without it in front of you." She adds, "I did and I flubbed it!" at the close of a wedding ceremony she was officiating. She says the bride's mother later laughed about it when they talked at the reception.

She remembers a funny incident when she was a pastor at the Rockland church. The church service was coming to an end and Cathie had set the communion elements on the floor next to the pulpit after communion had been served. A good-sized black bird, maybe a grackle, entered the church through the open doors at the back. The nave was a huge domed space with a center aisle. The bird hopped the length of the aisle, up onto the pulpit, jumped down, pecked the communion bread, and then hopped all the way back down the aisle.

The organist was behind a curtain and couldn't see the visitor, so the organ played on but all else was complete silence as the congregation observed the bird take communion, then fly off into the heavens. Cathie, in her clerical robe and collar at the front of the church, led the congregation in silent observation of the cheeky bird, grateful when it found its way out of the building rather than flying aimlessly trapped in the dome. One can guess there was great speculation that day as to what the bird signified.

Through the years Cathie has noticed that when she's conversing with a stranger who learns she is a minister, they explain their whole church history to her. Now that she no longer pastors a church, she feels freer to speak out, "to say what I need to. God's been chasing me around for some reason, so I say what I need to now."

Cathie offers some advice to women seeking a clerical life:

"If you feel the call, go for it. ... It's a privilege ... Sitting with people in a vet's office when they put down a family member ... it's an honor. ... When in church, you know people trust you pretty quickly if you're in the right place. ... You develop a deeper relationship not only with God but with people around you in the community." She believes her life "wouldn't have been as fulfilled" if she hadn't entered the ministry.

Regarding the need for women in ministry, Cathie speculates, "watching the evening news ... the world is going to need comfort ... sometimes women can provide more comfort than most men can. Maybe God sees that ... we're coming to a time when we need comfort." She sees this as one reason for so many more women entering the ministry these days, as the world gets tenser, more complicated, more in need of comfort.

At this time of her career Cathie serves people's spiritual needs in a somewhat different way than she did when she was a church pastor. She is the owner of Animal Rites, USA. The home page at www.animalritesusa.com says, "We understand pet owners just like us. We care for your needs when you really need us" and offers pet cremation services, memorial services which can be followed by a simple reception, a support group, and a candle-lighting ceremony.

Cathie ministers by either handling the process of putting down a loved pet—"family member"—accompanying the owner to the veterinarian's office, arranging a memorial of some kind, or offering support to a grieving owner after the death of a pet. This is a very serious ministry for her and she believes she has extended her church experience into a much-needed service for the many families who indeed consider their pets beloved family members. As Cathie says, "Once a minister, always a minister." The setting doesn't necessarily have to be a traditional church.

She was inspired to this ministry after the demise of their cat Sam. In 2001 Sam died after a lengthy illness that had reduced him to about two pounds of weight. When the ashes came back after his cremation, they weighed much more than Sam had. Upon investigation, Cathie learned that animals were not usually cremated individually and in fact she had received the ashes of several animals all cremated at the same time. This distressed her and also challenged her to find a solution.

Remembering her father's advice of many years earlier to "think about your own business" to work for herself and be independent, Cathie wondered if there was a service niche here for her. She investigated crematoriums that accepted pets until she located one that cremated in such a way that the ashes of each animal remain separate. For twelve years now, Cathie has been insuring that owners receive the ashes of their actual pets.

The business Animal Rites, the only one of its kind Cathie is aware of, is devoted to helping pet owners memorialize their family pets. She says, "When we take animals back [to the family after cremation], it's like they got their human back ... they feel whole again." She sees a growing tendency of families to treat their pets as family members, not just animals who live with them.

Animal Rites offers various services to owners. Cathie, often accompanied by Walter, picks up an animal after it has died, arranges for the cremation, and delivers the ashes to the pet owner, accompanied by a framed certificate including a lock of the animal's fur, and a nameplate. She includes a copy of an anonymous poem, "Rainbow Bridge," which describes the reuniting of owners and pets after death.

In the past she has offered grief support groups for those who have lost pets and periodic candlelight services for memorializing their pets. One family had several rescue birds and Cathie recalls the owner carrying the box of ashes of a beloved bird to a support group meeting and talking for an hour about her bird. Sometimes people put an obituary for an animal in the newspaper, and Cathie has on occasion referred owners to grief counselors in the community.

Animal Rites usually assists with dogs and cats but also deals with pet birds, an iguana, and once handled a goat. The business could not accommodate the request for cremation of an eight-hundred-pound pet cow but referred the owner to the National Zoo for assistance.

Cathie remembers the goat as requiring special effort because it lived "over the river and through the woods" quite literally. They had to walk over rocks and a stream to retrieve the goat's body from a hut surrounded by other goats, roll it up in a sort of soft sling carrier to transport it out, and carry it back through the natural obstacle course to get it into the vehicle to drive it to the crematorium.

They have handled a couple of two-hundred-seventy-five-pound mastiffs. One died on a mini-farm, and a little girl who lived there explained the chicken flock to Cathie while her dad brought out the huge dog in a wheelbarrow. In the other instance, the massive mastiff had been put down on the kitchen floor of the house, and they had to roll the two-hundred-seventy-five-pound dog into the one-hundred-fifty-pound-capacity carrying sling. "It took five or six of us to carry it up the uphill driveway," she says, and three men to unload it at the crematorium

Dog deaths sometimes occur in correspondence with other family trauma, such as an owner's surgery or death, happening "often enough that it's noticeable." Cathie recalls a time when a dog died in a bedroom in a house far off the highway, up a gravel road. The mother, father and children stood in a circle in the bedroom while the Pet Reverend said a prayer over the body of the dog. The next day the father went into the hospital for brain surgery.

She is very attentive to the needs of distressed families with pets. She says, "I feel like I'm helping people through the [grief] process. It makes me feel good because I feel like I'm helping them."

Her former work with a domestic violence center makes her aware that family abuse is often threatened toward or perpetrated against the family pet, also, and she sees the need for an abused woman and her children to be able to bring the family pet with them if they enter a shelter. Most confidential shelters do not include such accommodations.

Cathie says, "It is my dream to work with the city [Fredericksburg] to arrange shelters for people and their pets in the case of an emergency such as hurricane, tornado, or the like. Other areas of the country have had terrible disasters and people [with their pets] have had nowhere to go, so I am in the beginning stages of preparing a proposal to take to the proper officials in Fredericksburg to start the process of getting ready, just in case." Though pets are by law sheltered in a disaster, often they are not housed with their owners, a circumstance that some believe discourages people from entering shelters when they need the assistance.

With regard to her own ministry, she says, "I don't think it's over." Those requesting help from her with the final days of their pets surely must agree.

CHAPTER 6
Sarah

SARAH SMITH (PSEUDONYM), TWENTY-EIGHT, is pastor at a Lutheran Church (ELCA) in the South.

"Think carefully, pray boldly, and don't be a lone ranger." That's the advice Pastor Sarah, as she is called at her church, gives to women contemplating becoming clergywomen.

She practices all three in her daily life. For a young woman near the beginning of her career, Sarah has already had an amazing number of work and educational experiences. She has been a chaplain with Alzheimer's patients, worked in a public health clinic as an interpreter for Spanish-speaking clients, completed a unit of clinical pastoral education in an adolescent health and psych unit in a hospital, served as a youth leader, and has even done a stint as a bridal consultant. Each of these experiences gave her something to bring to her present role as pastor of a congregation, where she works with a senior pastor in a large ELCA church.

Sarah is a poised, confident-appearing woman with an engaging demeanor. She wears a pristine white clerical collar and black ministerial blouse, complemented by silver cuff earrings, bracelets and a dark purple sweater. She is used to people's reaction to her appearance and her youth, especially when older folks refer to her as a young or pretty pastor. She takes this in stride, realizing she is different from most pastors, though she clearly demonstrates remarkable achievement in other ways.

A native of a small town in the South, originally settled by German immigrants, Sarah grew up in a Missouri Synod Lutheran Church where she, her parents, and her older brother were very active. She attended a Lutheran primary school and a Southern Baptist high school ("hated it, like hated" the high school) and was "in the church pew every Sunday morning. Dad was an elder and Mom taught Sunday School." She was among the first group of girls who served as acolytes in her congregation but knew no female clergy growing up; the Missouri Synod of the Lutheran Church does not ordain women as pastors. She recalls, "I heard it [women pastors] talked negatively from the pulpit."

Sarah attended a college with Presbyterian ties, thinking about doing missions work, which she knew women were allowed to do. She majored in cross-cultural ministerial studies and remembers, "My parents were not excited by this." They feared her employment prospects might be limited.

She said her parents were very financially and practically minded and her dad may have hoped his daughter would follow him into his field of work. He advised that she needed a back-up study so she added Spanish to her curriculum and changed colleges to an affiliate school of the ELCA. She majored in religion and family ministry and minored in Spanish, graduating summa cum laude. She also received a prestigious award for excellence in religious studies.

Conversations with her parents became strained and "very

distant at times" as she pursued her studies, Sarah recalls. When she told her mother she wanted to become a pastor, her mother intoned, "Get thee behind me, Satan," in response. Sarah says, "There was quite a schism in the Smith household. However, we've both learned a lot since then."

Although her parents took some persuading, Sarah always felt support from her grandmothers. She believes they were more progressive and accepted the idea of her ordination better than anyone else in her family. One grandmother was a secretary in an ELCA church and remembers the young child Sarah sneaking into the empty sanctuary at her grandmother's church and "playing church." Sarah laughs and says, "I take after my grandmothers."

She thought about pursuing a doctorate and becoming a professor of theology at a Lutheran college. She had loved her undergraduate theology study and others, primarily professors, had told her she had the makings of a pastor. However, in her early twenties, deciding what to do about a career, she still had had no interaction with female Lutheran pastors.

Her professors encouraged her to continue her religious studies. She felt called to be a pastor but her understanding of scripture, plus the things she'd seen and been taught as a child, told her she couldn't do that. She says, "At that time, I felt I had to obey a call from God to go into ministry but I was struggling to make sure the call was truly one from God, because thus far in my faith formation and biblical understanding, my sense of call and my understanding of God were incompatible. And my sense of call and current theology resulted in a time of stirring."

Sarah entered the divinity school at a prominent Southern university, a school with historical ties to the Baptist church, where she earned a master of divinity degree. She recalls, "The school was a mix of varied denominations with a good representation of racial and sexual orientation diversity. It was a place that aimed to be safe for everyone. It stretched me a lot. The seminary was just a great place for me." Although there were still more men than women, she had many female fellow classmates. She calls them "dear and sacred colleagues, then and now more than ever," and says they get together for annual visits and virtual gatherings.

Her seminary years were a time of clarification for her. "I knew once I got to seminary, I was answering God's call," she says. "Though it hurt to say goodbye to my [Missouri Synod] church, I couldn't say no anymore. I felt like Moses looking for an Aaron or Miriam," after she heard from several of her professors that she belonged in the pastorate. One professor in particular, a legally blind man who could barely see the red shoes she often wore, told her, "Ladybug, you're going to be a pastor."

After receiving her master's degree from this university, Sarah enrolled in a Lutheran seminary where she received a second master's degree, this one in sacred theology. Here Sarah says she put feminist theology together with Lutheran theology.

Sarah has been in her current church for several years. She came as an intern— a vicar—but was subsequently called by the church as a pastor. She and the senior pastor share the roles of preaching and pastoral care, and Sarah loves the call. She says she is thankful to be in a healthy church and on a healthy leadership team. "We laugh a lot and share preaching and pastoral care. Each Sunday, one pastor presides and one preaches. I preside and preach equally."

Some clergywomen find themselves in a non-healthy situation in jobs clergymen may turn down, the only places the women may be able to find employment. Sarah comments, "Sexism still exists in the pews" and notes that "the sanctuary is not as safe for women" who sometimes face assaults or sexist comments. Sarah says she is aware of this possibility "but not paranoid about it" and feels blessed with her current assignment.

The ELCA branch of the Lutheran church welcomes female clergy. Salary differentials between women and men, Sarah says, are more likely to be due to differences in assignments. Women are more likely to be called as part-time pastors and men are more likely to be senior pastors in the larger churches, a reflection of the larger culture, not of any guidelines within the ELCA. The synod sets guidelines for compensation, providing for some parity in salaries. Currently the presiding Bishop of the ELCA is a clergywoman, Rev. Elizabeth A. Eaton, elected to the post in 2013 by the Churchwide Assembly.

Among Sarah's other duties is working with the college students at a nearby university, a ministry shared jointly by her church and one of another denomination. She especially enjoys her work with the younger youth at her church. One of her best memories so far was taking a group of middle and high school students to a national youth conference in Detroit. One day in the exhibit hall, the youngest member of her group was standing in front of an exhibit on immigration from Central America. Sarah says, "He looked like he didn't get it. Then he said, 'I think our country doesn't have a conscience.' I felt God's spirit moving him."

Her other joys and moving moments occur during pastoral visits, especially to hospital patients. She says, "I find holy moments, especially at funerals. I see the cross." She sees others' bold faith and their hurts and says, "I feel God's promise to me. For Lutherans, God acts in suffering chiefly in the cross, so it is in the suffering of death or loss that we are most confident in God's mighty action in Christ."

Sarah says about her current life, "Planting roots has been very hard. There is a college but not a young professional community in this city. I've had to be very intentional. I can make friends like that, but I've had to be intentional here."

She has dated someone for two years and says, "Most friends at home don't understand why I don't have a husband and children, why I'm not a teacher like they are. They consistently support me but don't understand why I can't come home, for example, just because there's a funeral at my church. I don't have the energy to convince them and it's not related to their salvation. So I just let people be where they are. I don't have to be Pastor Sarah to them."

If she hadn't taken the path she has, she speculates that she might have married. "Female clergy have to make decisions. I'd have gone on to my Ph.D. and been active in church. I knew my full God-given creativity, gifts, worth, were dismissed by my [childhood] denomination. Not just me, all the other women. I couldn't worship there.

"Being a clergywoman has opened my eyes to the joys and despairs of life," Sarah says. "When you're a congregational leader, you're up close and personal, you learn more about people's lives. You see God most in suffering. I've seen God move lives. Sometimes you become so extended, you need to step back and observe your own religious rituals, trust one of the few places left in society where intimacy is a natural response. The pastor and parishioner relationship is one of the few places left in society where there is a relationship of trust. What other professional do you invite into your home?"

She says she rarely feels frustrated in her jobs, then laughs and says, "Well, maybe mundane meetings." She says one has to learn when "to be a proclaimer, prophet, discern when to be prophetic and when a comforter." She says clergy must learn when to "move slowly, even if that means inching forward, or when to run with all your might."

Sarah calls herself a "pipe-liner" in her career, doing exactly what she believes she was called to do. "I am at such a high place in my life." However, she has some cautions for other women contemplating the clergy. She says finances can be a real stumbling block and potential clergy need to be prepared for debt repayment.

She adds, "A pretty face on a young female has its own challenges. People are not always as ready to see a female's body ... intellect, yes, you have to be smarter. But society has always felt possessive of the female body and we are not always our own persons. I had to learn how to be open, hospitable, but protective of what is rightfully mine." She believes organizations should be webs, not ladders or pyramids. She said, "I hope to be serving, whether thirty or three thousand, always to be relational."

Sarah concludes with some words to readers of this book. "Thank you to those of you reading the book if you're reading trying to understand, even if you vehemently disagree. Bold cheerleaders and prayer warriors, get up with us, believe, serve, worship with us."

CHAPTER 7
Brenda

BRENDA BILER, FIFTY-EIGHT, WAS ordained as a pastor in the United Methodist Church at the age of thirty. She is currently a senior pastor at Fredericksburg United Methodist Church in Virginia.

When Brenda decided to attend seminary and went home to tell her parents, her mother said, "Your father thinks you're making a very big mistake." Thirty years of ordination have shown her decision to enter the ministry to be correct, a decision her parents eventually accepted. "Religion has not helped pull our family together," she comments.

Brenda presents a very professional image, in a stylish black dress with a black and white sweater, heels and stockings, and a long necklace of white beads. She sits in an upholstered chair in a conversation area of her spacious office with book-lined walls. She is unusual in her denomination — and among other denominations, as well —because she is a clergywoman in a senior pastorate of a large, historic church of 2,500 members.

Faith was always important in Brenda's life, though during her childhood, religion was a point of contention in her household.

One parent was Methodist, the other Roman Catholic. She grew up attending the Catholic church at least once each year with her grandmother and from that experience, developed a sense of awe. She saw the Methodist church of her childhood as "more chatty" when the congregation gathered and thinks the combination helped give her balance of God's transcendent and immanent attributes, allowing for a richer understanding of the Holy.

She received her bachelor's degree from Allegheny College in Meadville, PA, with a joint major in political science and biology. Allegheny College is a small liberal arts school historically affiliated with the Methodist Church, though today it is non-sectarian. One of the oldest colleges in the U.S. and one of the earliest to admit women, it was a logical educational cradle for a woman who has emerged as a leader in her denomination.

After finishing college, Brenda held jobs that provided services to people in need. She was hired to adjudicate black-lung cases in a program in a new office that was just getting organized. From this experience she learned how to navigate a bureaucracy and how to be an administrator as she developed forms and processes. She became a caseworker in the office of the late Congressman Carl Perkins, a Kentucky Democrat known for supporting education and services for the underprivileged.

While she worked on Capitol Hill, she sought a church to attend and tried both Methodist and Baptist congregations. After attending a Methodist service, she received postcards and remembers them written in red ink from a member of the Evangelical Committee of the church. She decided "to give the Methodists another try." She got very involved in her church in Crystal City, VA, and found a mentor in an associate pastor there. She realized her vocation while she was in her early twenties.

She says, "I'd always been sensitive to people's faith journeys and had a deeper hunger to understand the church. I could see people in need, often people of faith." However, the merger of a majority of the Evangelical United Brethren Church (EUB) and Methodist denominations resulted in the United Methodist Church in 1968 and the subsequent split in the church of her childhood. Thus Brenda was not baptized until her mid-twenties, when she was active in a United Methodist congregation. This church would eventually be the community where she would be nurtured in the faith and receive her call to ordained ministry.

"I had a hunger, a quest that continued to grow," she says. She had expected to go to graduate school but didn't know what field she'd pursue. She was in "searching and seeking mode" when at Annual Conference (a Methodist yearly gathering of clergy and lay members to worship and conduct church business together), she had a "strong sense of God saying, 'It's okay if you don't go to seminary, but what are you afraid of?'" At that point she had never seen a female minister and knew only one woman who had even applied to seminary.

The first time she spoke of her call to ministry, she confided in a Roman Catholic Capitol Hill colleague. "I think I'm being called to ministry." The woman did not recoil at the revelation, so Brenda felt encouraged. "This whole idea of a call—it's not on the phone, written in the clouds ... there's nothing tangible," she explains. "God's call was talked about in scripture but I don't recall a sermon or a conversation about the experience of call in one's own life."

She planned to begin seminary as a part-time student while she worked in Congress, but the sudden death of Congressman Perkins altered her plan. Her church hired her as an assistant to the minister. They paid a small salary that covered her health insurance and she lived in a parsonage. "I wore a [clerical] stole, less formal rules then"—and learned about the inner workings of the church before she ever went to seminary. She remembers those years with "a very invitational congregation." This congregation elected her as co-lay-leader, prior to her call to ministry. Through that leadership position and others, Brenda learned much about the organization of a local church.

A less invitational experience occurred at her first Annual Conference at the Hotel Roanoke, which she attended as an observer at the invitation of a lay delegate. This was Brenda's first experience of the "larger church." Attendees wore different-colored name badges to denote status as clergy, lay leaders, and other designations. Brenda remembers being on the elevator wearing a badge-less red silk dress when a male clergyman asked her, "Are you clergy? A spouse? Who are you?" She thought the question very rude. At that conference she saw some clergywomen and thought, "They look normal."

When a pastor asked her what she thought of her first conference, she replied, "Not much," and explained that she'd "like to divide the clergymen into groups where they could be taught some manners. They need to be aware of what others see." She still sees occasional differences in how male and female clergy are treated, though she believes younger women in the ministry "feel more equality and I hope it's always there for them. I don't believe we're there yet. It's sometimes subtle, but not always." She believes there's still a "stained-glass ceiling for women."

Her seminary class was about half female, but not all the women became ordained. Brenda commuted to seminary and worked and remembers it as a hectic time in her life. Her seminary class became her support group for her first appointment as a minister, a church she pastored for four years. The first year of her appointment was the final year of her studies at Wesley

Theological Seminary in Washington, DC, where she earned her master of divinity degree.

The United Methodist Church began ordaining women to the ministry in 1956. Brenda was first ordained as a deacon, then as an elder three years later. The United Methodist Church website describes an elder as being ordained to preach, teach, provide pastoral care and counseling, and administer the sacraments of baptism and communion. Elders are itinerant and appointed to their positions. They move to a new church or other position whenever they are told by their bishop to do so.

At the time of Brenda's ordination, United Methodist pastors were ordained twice, first as a deacon, a probationary relationship, and then as an elder. In 1996 this practice changed and those on the "elder track" are now commissioned in a provisional relationship and then ordained. An order of deacon was established in 1996 for clergy who are called to bridge the church and the world.

Brenda has been a pastor in five different churches for a total of twenty-one years. She served as an administrator in a district superintendent's office for eight years before being appointed to her current church. After she had been a pastor for eleven years in two different churches, she yearned to explore her call more deeply.

"I'm a person that loves administration, organizations and systems. That makes me a bit unusual in the profession," she says. "I thought I'd like to teach church administration because I didn't feel that was being well taught," but she discovered there is not a degree program in church administration. Desiring a doctorate, she didn't want to enroll in a doctorate of ministry program. She became a part-time doctoral student in the Public Policy and Administration program at Virginia Commonwealth University in Richmond. She received her Ph.D. there in 2001.

Brenda enjoyed the "fascinating cross-section of people in my doctoral classes. They became a supportive community." She was the only pastor in the group and says in some ways that gave her more opportunity to share her faith with some of her cohorts who were frustrated with traditional religion. She officiated at a wedding of one of the group. At that busy time of graduate school, she really began to understand the notion of "retreat" as restorative time, taking a week off and being secluded for a time of spirituality, time she increasingly has trouble finding.

At an Annual Conference, a clergywoman questioned the bishop about why so many women were being ordained but not going into church positions. Brenda discovered there was no record-keeping on attrition of clergy. She was on a Women in Ministry Task Force and resigned from that committee "to do the legwork for a study" with the Center for Public Policy at VCU in 1997, which led to her dissertation topic. Reaching people for interviews was difficult since there were no records, but the researchers had "fascinating personal interviews" with twenty-one clergywomen and nine clergymen, leading to a survey of a large number of clergy who were employed in Virginia.

They discovered systemic issues for both men and women in ministry. However, there were also significant differences between the men and women responding to the survey almost twenty years ago, including these: Clergywomen earned less, moving often was more problematic for women, women felt under-utilized and under-appreciated, women became less committed to parish ministry over time, and they felt the ministry had a less positive impact on their marriages. Overall, the report concluded, clergywomen were more likely to leave ministry than clergymen. This research experience further fueled Brenda's interest in church administration and in equality for clergywomen.

This research led directly to her dissertation, *The Effects of Respondent Characteristics and Exit, Voice, and Loyalty Cues in a Clergy Workforce: Identifying Organizational Relapse and Offering Remedies for Repair* (VCU, 2001). She concluded that organizations, including churches, need to pay attention to "exit and voice behavior cues"—in other words, listen to their folks, especially the unhappy ones.

Brenda has continued her theoretical and practical work in church organization throughout her various ministerial assignments. She notes that expectations for clergy are totally different now than they were twenty years ago: "Everyone wants everything right now. You're always on—entertainment and popularity are part of ministry. Spirituality is hard work. We're not 'instant people.' People have the idea, 'That's what we're paying you for.' A better question is 'How do we all use our gifts?'"

She says the importance of community leadership in the church is emerging more strongly, particularly dependent on the size of the church. A small church is more likely to be matriarchal/patriarchal, pastoral care-centered; a larger one, ministry-centered; then in the biggest churches, a corporate model emerges. It's important for a church to transition from the pastor and staff doing all the work to a church where everyone is engaged in ministry. This kind of systemic change is a long and tedious process, but "If we are effective persons and systems persons, we can do better ministry." She cites the example of John Wesley, founder of the Methodist Church in the 1700s, who was not known as a great preacher but was an effective organizer.

Her clerical life is "a gift because it challenges me to read more, pray more, see life through a different lens than I otherwise would have had. God's made me a captive audience and I wrestle with things that I never would have." When she became a pastor some of her friends were curious but she found opportunities to talk about faith with others.

She finds it hard to set priorities because there's always something to do, something new to learn. The best part of her job is that no two days are alike, there are always surprises, and it's never boring. She loves being with people in a "really sacred space, being present when they struggle, not fixing things but representing Christ in the church."

Brenda continues, "I've never felt separated from God in my ministry. However, there have been times that I've not understood what God is wanting me to see, learn, or experience. In the midst of those difficult times, by God's grace, I have trusted that God was with me. They have turned out to be some of the richest experiences in my life and ministry."

She laments, "My inbox is never empty. I need to let go of the fact that I'll get it all done." For her, writing sermons and conducting worship are very different from day-to-day pastoral care. Every day has different elements and "Aspects of every day are very difficult." She recently enjoyed that she "rang the bell for Appomattox" to commemorate peace achieved there one hundred fifty years ago.

To women going into the ministry, Brenda advises, "Don't be a victim. It's a profession. Seek out other persons, don't feel like you have to do it alone. I can call any variety of people, both male and female," though she notes it's harder to find women in large churches such as her present assignment to compare notes with.

If she had it to do over again, Brenda would become a pastor. "I followed the call, was compelled, yet an invitation, not pushed into it. I felt loved by God." As a pastor, "You see things differently, how we run the church, what's God's vision for this church, will wrestle with that fascinating journey."

She explains how she uses a discerning process for the church to answer this question, using surveys of congregational perceptions. If she had not become a clergywoman, she would have been very involved in social action in another way. "I believe God continues to call us. God's call doesn't stop with ordination."

Her life now is complicated by the fact that her mother is in a nursing home and she provides support for her father: "I call him daily." On her days off she goes home to Pennsylvania where she writes checks and generally gets things organized for the next month. Essentially she has no time off at present. She says the bishop urges ministers to take "renewal time" and notes, "I take responsibility for not clearing my calendar and unplugging."

She says her job can be lonely: "I am introverted and get energy from quiet, private time. I don't have time to do basic things I need to do for me. I don't have a weekend, don't get a holiday," and says she has no time to build a support system at present. She is in a very demanding job, an unusual role as a female senior in a very large church with four services on Sunday and over a thousand attending services on Easter Sunday. She sees forty-five to fifty-five as the prime age range for major assignments and is herself beyond that age so doesn't see her future clearly.

Brenda reminds us that "Wherever God is calling you is an opportunity. That is our witness, to use the ordinary events of life to witness Christ," whether in church or not. "We don't all have to be the same. Every living person is different—ministers are as diverse as other populations, a reflection of who God is."

CHAPTER 8

Torrence

TORRENCE HARMAN, SEVENTY-ONE, IS the rector of St. Mary's Whitechapel and Trinity Episcopal Churches in Lancaster, VA, and adjunct faculty at Rappahannock Community College.

"I get tired of hearing the emphasis on the hereafter. It hijacks the present. I believe Jesus' message is to live in the here and now. The yet-to-come you [will] live into."

This assertion epitomizes Torrence's approach to her busy life as she involves herself in myriad ways in the church and the community. She jokes that she is not a type-A but rather a "triple-A personality."

She pastors two yoked Episcopal churches, leads discernment committees for persons contemplating vocations in the Episcopal church, has served on many diocesan committees, and is a spiritual director assisting others to find deeper meaning in their lives. She invites young people to examine their own beliefs as she teaches religion courses at a community college. She has close relationships with her family, friends, and colleagues, and seems to know most Episcopalians in Virginia.

Torrence looks serene in a loose-fitting white blouse, black knit slacks and black flats. White hair haloes her face. She manages to be both voluble and attentive simultaneously and seems always present and focused on whomever she's talking to. As Southerners say, she never misses a trick. She is plagued with arthritis and scoliosis but works long hours, often traveling some distance in her serviceable old Ford Focus to arrive at her next meeting of the day.

Her early years helped prepare her for her current calling, but Torrence did not aspire to become a priest and did not know any female clergy when she was a child. She is a cradle Episcopalian, a lifelong member of the church. Her parents divorced when she was two years old, and she and her mother lived with her grandparents until she was seven, when her mother remarried. Three siblings soon followed, but Torrence remained very connected with her grandparents. Her grandfather was an Episcopal priest and she participated in church activities regularly.

She recalls that time as somewhat confusing, saying, "I was never really sure of my place in all the family dynamics going on around me."

She attended St. Catherine's, an Episcopal girls' school in Richmond, for her elementary and high school years. She remembers a time as a teenager sitting on the green at St. Catherine's and watching girls bullying another student. "I watched and felt the urge to stand up and do something. I didn't." The recollection of this experience is still with her and she decided as an adult to stand up and do something, a decision that shaped her career choices.

She was married in the Episcopal Church to a young lawyer and had three children by the time she was twenty-six years old. She did volunteer work as a young woman with women's organizations, with St. Paul's Episcopal Church, which she and her family attended in downtown Richmond, and with other civic groups with a primary interest in social justice issues. During this period, she decided to go back to college, earning a bachelor of science in business administration and management.

"These were incredibly busy years, raising three children, keeping up with their activities while working in the community and then finishing college. I basically worked around the children's schedules and home life. Thank goodness I had a lot of energy," Torrence recalls.

After working with the representatives of several women's organizations lobbying for juvenile justice issues, she decided she might be a more focused and effective advocate if she got a law degree. "I vowed I was going to go into a place where I can stand up and help make a difference in others' lives one at a time." She received the juris doctor degree in 1983 from University of Richmond Law School.

She and her husband separated in the middle of her second year. She became a lawyer when she was thirty-nine years old, remaining an active member of the Virginia bar for about twenty years. She is still a member of the state bar but shifted to associate status in 2007. She said, "I know God called me into law for purposes known only unto God."

Torrence became a very successful lawyer. About four years into her legal career—very early for such an overture—she was approached about becoming a candidate for a judgeship, but she decided her place was being a lawyer. "I'm not meant to judge people. I'm meant to be with people, one, two or a small group. I know that. I understand the tugs and pulls someone goes through."

She was a family law attorney in a small practice—the only female partner—and was certified as a mediator by the Virginia

Supreme Court. She was voted by her peers as one of the "Best Lawyers in Virginia" in the 1990s, was active with bar committees and ultimately served as the chair of the Board of Governors of the Family Law Section of the Virginia State Bar in 1999.

This very demanding legal career was also very rewarding to her during her twenty years as a mediator. However, she notes, "I felt increasing dis-ease with law and even mediation because of the extremely hostile and demanding type of law and mediation I did, family law and divorce mediation. I was beginning to feel burnout coming on as well as resisting the work. I deeply desired to do something that didn't seem to destroy relationships, but rather build them."

Things took a major turn in her life after her mother was diagnosed with cancer, dying two years later. She found herself drawn towards a deeper examination of her life and faith, which she explored more intentionally when she attended an Education for Ministry (EFM) program at her church with her husband, Buff. This is Torrence's second marriage and they have been married for thirty years. She calls her EFM time "a match made in heaven" in terms of decision-making for her call to ministry in the church instead of continuing in the law. EFM is an intense multi-year theological education of small-group study and introduced her to theological and deeper reflection on her life.

"We did a graph and timeline with events and relationship with the Divine. It was very much an aha moment for me. I realized when I'd most experienced God was in the low times, when I found Him, when He found me. The low points, that's when I was cracked open. That's when I found the connection with God, who was always with me."

Torrence recalls, "I didn't know I was called to be a priest. I knew I was called to attend seminary." She received the master of divinity degree from Union Presbyterian Seminary in Richmond, and a certificate of studies from Virginia Theological Seminary in Alexandria. She was ordained an Episcopal priest at the age of sixty.

Her reaction to seminary was, "I loved it!" She had a strong support group of friends, study partners, and male and female classmates. "Several faculty members, especially some female faculty, were, I believe, instrumental and extremely supportive in my journey."

She is also a graduate of the two-year Spiritual Guidance Program at Shalem Institute in Washington, which describes itself as an organization providing "in-depth support for contemplative living and leadership—a way of being in the world that is prayerfully attentive and responsive to God's presence and guidance" for people from many different denominations and faith traditions (www.shalem.org). Of Shalem and the contemplative approach to religious thinking, she says, "My world has turned around and my life is so much richer."

Her Shalem experience led her to be a spiritual director for other individuals for the past four years. "Sitting with people and seeing the Spirit move in their lives is the most amazing gift ever," she says. "It's where I see moment-to-moment presence, God's desire for us unfolding. It has astounded me, is an ongoing transformation in my life."

Prior to ordination, in 2002 Torrence spent about nine months as a seminarian, an intern, at Trinity Episcopal Church in Fredericksburg, during the time of the killings in the area by Beltway Snipers John Allen Muhammad and Lee Boyd Malvo. She knew the attorneys who represented the younger shooter and in a later sermon used a portion of the attorney's closing argument in which he convinced the jury not to award the death penalty. The attorney had referenced the story in John 8:7 in which Jesus told the crowd about to stone a woman, "Let anyone who is without sin cast the first stone."

She did the same sort of teaching at her own church after the Boston Marathon bombing, asking people to consider how the bleeding young man felt huddled in the boat where he had hidden after the event. She attempted to get people to experience the young man's fear, the struggle of doing what his older brother had told him to. When asked to pray for those they considered enemies, a couple of parishioners objected to the sermon, to which she replied, "He's a boy and God asks us to pray for our enemies!" She added, "As a lawyer or a priest, I've never felt anyone would attack me," but she felt the need to respond to others in her congregations who felt fear from crime.

After ordination, Torrence was called as assistant rector at St. James' Episcopal Church in midtown Richmond, a large urban church of 2,500 parishioners. Her responsibilities included adult Christian education/formation and pastoral care. These are among her favorite parts of work as a clergywoman, as well as preaching, teaching and outreach. She finds administrative work the least interesting, especially "reports and truly clerical [not in a clergy sense] work that falls far too often on the rector of a small church."

For the past eight years she has been rector of two small yoked Episcopal churches in Lancaster County. Each of her churches has a membership of eighty to ninety people, with usual Sunday attendance about forty to fifty people. St. Mary's Whitechapel Episcopal Church, a historic colonial church, was founded in 1669 and is located near Lively, VA. Those attending range mostly from sixty to ninety years of age and include a Jesuit priest and retired Presbyterian and Methodist ministers. "The people there," says Torrence, "are a wealth of knowledge."

Their younger sister church, Trinity Episcopal of Lancaster, founded in 1884, lies about six miles away. Trinity's website describes a "Little Church with a Big Heart ... growing with new members of all ages. Folks come as they are, gathering together for worship, friendship, and community." Godly play for young people and nursery care are listed on the website (www.trinitylancasterva.org).

Torrence and her husband now live in Lancaster, a small town in the Northern Neck area of Virginia, where her two churches are located. They moved from the city of Richmond to a cottage in this more rural area, which they renovated. Torrence describes adjusting to the rural area and enlarging the cottage, saying with a laugh, "I asked both congregations to pray for our marriage during the renovation. We needed their prayers. Our wills clash when we renovate."

She commented on advice she gave to a new deacon at the two churches, "You don't go in your clerical collar to drink a martini [in a small town], not in the corner bar in Lively, Virginia." She enjoys the quiet and natural beauty of the rural area on the Rappahannock River where it empties into the Chesapeake Bay.

She has been well accepted in her role as female priest in a denomination that has ordained women for forty years. Regarding others' reactions, she says, "Family and friends have been very positive. A few male colleagues and/or a very traditional male or female parishioner may be negative about female clergy in general, may have been standoffish and 'discounting,' or even negative and oppositional at time, but these types have been generally very few."

Torrence says, "I have often felt that what bolstered [positive] perception of me was their knowledge that I had been for twenty years, not only an attorney but a successful and well-regarded one in my profession, both locally and statewide." She says, "The priesthood has used my existing skills and gifts and stretched me, honed me, and refined those skills and gifts, helped me live into newer ones, and sustained, pruned and yielded new fruitfulness in me."

Through the years Torrence has learned to listen to herself and believes we need to "listen to our bodies, our hearts. They tell us when things are getting out of sync. Alignment is a significant issue in my life." She explains that she has scoliosis, so alignment is an important fact and metaphor for her. "I desire alignment, energy moving through. I can see patterns, feel the flow of energy. I can see patterns in another's life."

She discerned her call to ministry "through a lot of prayer, conversations with God and several friends and family members. I felt my life moving closer and closer into relationship/alignment with the movement of the Holy Spirit in my life." She adds, "The discernment of where God wants to use one is the gift of years, experience. I have to distinguish among voices, to be aware of my body, my heart and my feelings. I feel something, stop, then move into my head and reconcile the two, heart and mind. The orientation to be self-aware is a saving grace in my life."

When asked if there have been times when she has felt separated from God, a spiritual bleakness, especially related to her ministry, she replies, "Yes." She explains, "I feel distanced from God at times when something in myself or in the world around me blocks me from connection with God or with others. When I get into my head too much or want to control outcomes or find myself reacting negatively to expectations. That's why the practice of self-awareness is so critical in my life, and good friends who will call me on it." Meditation, sitting by the river that flows in front of her house, talking to her spiritual director, seeking out a clergy friend, taking intentional "time-outs" particularly in nature, and simply quieting down are strategies she uses to handle times like these. "What a relief, God's always waiting for me," she says.

Her sense of humor is apparent as she relates a time when she forgot to turn off her cell phone during a Sunday service. Amidst the candles and music, "My damn cell phone went off." She held it up to the congregation and said, "Hello, God, God's calling us. Everybody say hello to God." Then she switched off her phone and never did learn who was on the phone that morning. Since then she has remembered to silence her phone before services.

Torrence believes some passages in the Bible "started me thinking. Sin is distance from God, distance from your neighbor and your true self. However, everyone is loved, found by God. We're the ones who turned our back on God, put too much distance between me and my true self-trajectory."

She continues, "When I get too far from self, I feel the gap. My desire to get back in alignment makes a magnetic field that draws me back. The sign of the Spirit is tenderness, a sense of being held, oneness with vulnerability."

Helping some discern their clerical calling and others develop their own spirituality are particularly satisfying for Torrence. Within the diocese she leads carefully selected groups of parishioners at churches around the diocese who meet with a candidate in the process of discerning a call for the vocational deaconate or the priesthood. This committee, trained and initially led by Torrence, helps the candidate explore whether or not she or he has a calling for vocational life. Through spiritual direction Torrence helps those seeking a deeper spiritual life to find their way. In both instances, "We enter the river of community. As a group, we go down and tap into Source, a deep mystical place where the questions the Spirit wants considered arise."

One aspect of her service Torrence particularly enjoys is teaching Old and New Testament courses and a course named "Religions in America" to community college students at Rappahannock Community College. She believes many young people today are disillusioned by organized religion. When she asks, "Why would you leave the church?" she hears answers such as, 'My pastor had an affair and didn't look godly anymore,' or 'He's just an old white guy,' or 'Everybody fights in the church.' They don't just reject the pastor, they reject religion."

She tries to get them to think in larger terms by asking questions such as, "Religion in America—how does it affect you every day? Why is what is happening in the Middle East important here? Our worldwide global village, how do you get your news? How is the Constitution working in the U.S. regarding separation of church and state?"

When asked what advice she'd give to women contemplating becoming clergywomen, Torrence quickly responds, "I don't give advice. I would ask them questions. What's going on? What's stirring within you? Try to move them away from practical questions at first, rather get them to discern how the Spirit may be moving in their life. I'm a firm believer that a person best knows the solution in their lives if they stop and take time to listen within themselves. A fix-it mentality is so prevalent. Seminary has helped me understand, be present, listen. My role is to listen and help them uncover what's inside them."

She noted that men more often become priests in the largest Episcopal churches, the canon churches, where they are expected to be CEOs as well as pastors. Women find employment in smaller churches, perhaps yoked churches such as she serves, or in bi-vocational positions, meaning holding another job while serving as clergy. Regarding female clergy, she notes, "We're more likely to over-function. Even if one is part-time, we work more than that." She has talked to many women who are interested in becoming either lawyers or clergy, professions more women are entering but where men are still prevalent, particularly in prestigious, visible positions.

In the little spare time she has, Torrence enjoys writing, especially poetry. Her parents both wrote for prominent newspapers in earlier years and she has inherited their affinity for words. She confides, "I have folders and folders of poetry written through the years." She seeks the quiet of contemplation for her thinking and writing. She also enjoys gardening, homemaking, and spending time with her family, including her grandchildren, and with friends. She reads voraciously.

The Episcopal Church requires that clergy retire at the age of seventy-two, so Torrence faces mandatory retirement soon. She has done much thinking about how to fashion her life in the coming years, although she knows the denomination's strict rules regarding participation in a parish where one has been priest will make a difference in her life, particularly in a small town. She says she has experienced "aging discernment and anticipatory grief" as she's thought about the losses retirement will bring. "I experienced real grieving for several months last year but I have gotten much stronger. The loss is not as traumatic as I thought it would be. God's helping me relax about this."

Torrence is feeling a "real draw into outreach." She says she's never felt she was good at asking people for money, but has lately helped put together funds within the congregation to support a local effort to send kids to a regional Boys and Girls Club summer camp program. "I thought, I'm going to make this happen.

This matters." She anticipates moving into meaningful activity in her community.

"Authenticity is so critical now. People can gut-spot it in a second." Torrence's absolute authenticity will lead her into the future, serving her well as it has in the past. She concludes confidently, "I'm excited abut retirement." Likely everyone will want this triple-A-type retired priest on their team.

CHAPTER 9
Tanya

TANYA YOUNG, SIXTY-EIGHT, IS authorized by the State of North Carolina to officiate at weddings and other ceremonies.

Tanya is part of the burgeoning industry of destination weddings and the destination she represents is the beautiful Outer Banks coastal area of North Carolina. She designs wedding services for couples committed to a life together. She herself comes from a traditional Christian background, but writes either religious or secular vows for her clients. "I feel we all believe in something greater than ourselves—a Source, whatever."

Her business card reads, "Outer Banks Wedding Ceremony, Reverend Tanya K. Young, Non-Denominational Minister." Her website announces, "Congratulations! My name is Reverend Tanya Young and I would be honored to be a part of your wedding day here on the Outer Banks of North Carolina."

A woman with a polished, professional appearance and a friendly but business-like demeanor, Tanya has dark short hair tipped with golden highlights. She wears a white top over slacks, short dangling earrings, beachy sandals, well-manicured rose-colored fingernails, turquoise toenails and a large gold ring on her left hand, the epitome of tasteful hip beach fashion. She comes to the interview with a typed-out list of points she wants to cover.

By law in North Carolina, only magistrates or ordained ministers can perform marriage ceremonies. Magistrates typically perform ceremonies in the courthouse. Tanya became ordained in 2003 on-line through an organization called Universal Ministries, a process approved within North Carolina regulations. When she entered the ministry and the wedding business at Outer Banks in the early 2000s, she recalls maybe eight people doing such independent services. Now there are about forty independent wedding ministers in the area.

About half the time, Tanya does not meet the couples she marries "before they're in front of me." Contact and planning occur through her website and the telephone. She says a couple and their families usually rent an "event home," one or more of the huge many-bedroom, many-bathroom rental properties that line the Outer Banks shoreline. Clients come from far and near to this "destination wedding" site. Tanya says they usually stay for a week, arriving on Saturday or Sunday, getting their marriage license on Monday, and holding the wedding on Tuesday or Wednesday. The rest of their week they enjoy the beach destination as their honeymoon.

All her life she's been a self-described entrepreneur. Tanya is almost a native of the area; she was just three years old when her family relocated to the Outer Banks from Greensboro, NC. Her father was a realtor and businessman in the 1950s, who first developed Avalon Beach in the Kill Devil Hills area of the Outer Banks. At that time the hospitality industry in the area consisted of small hotels and cottages. She recalls, "I was checking people into and out of cottages when I was ten years old. Real estate was a service industry then. I've always been in customer service."

She was gone from the area during the '90s working for corporate hotel chains and returned in the early 2000s when the wedding industry began to take off. She believed there was a place for her as an entrepreneur in that niche, but decided she wasn't a caterer or a photographer. She said most of the weddings at that time were "cookie-cutter ceremonies with little input from the couple. I saw the need for a more creative and inclusive approach, incorporating all religions and also non-religions." Tanya researched wedding ceremonies on-line, both religious and secular, and educated herself about the possibilities. She'd always enjoyed writing and envisioned the ceremonies she could create for couples.

"I began writing from the heart, particularly about love," she says. "I saw myself as a vessel to interpret what they wish to promise on their wedding day and also helping couples to create a ceremony that reflected them. I started writing ceremonies and giving couples choices. This was embraced and my business was launched in 2003."

Developing a ceremony that pleases a couple and their families takes some skill and discretion. Sometimes a couple will say, "Got to have some religion because of family. Then I include a prayer or a blessing." She notes that nobody really notices a non-religious ceremony in twenty minutes on a beautiful beach: "Most people won't realize there's no prayer or other religious references."

Sometimes couples want their pets incorporated into the ceremony and often a ceremony includes the bride's or groom's children, or maybe both. Her website says, "It is my belief that second marriages and blended families deserve the same care and reverence as the first one. I often add special additions for children … you may choose to present them with a small gift—a necklace or ring or something that is an important family statement."

Tanya was raised a Methodist in Kitty Hawk Village, in a "simple and loving religion, a peaceful religion." When she was a young mother with two daughters, she moved away from religion but later attended the Episcopal church, which seemed to call to her and her children. She says, "I liked the ritual and found it very inclusive."

She now considers herself very spiritual and attends conferences, such as the "Celebrate Your Life" conference held by Mishka Productions in Chicago in June 2015, to "fill myself up." She finds the spiritual community "somewhat hidden here. I also attend Hay House Conferences led by Louise Hay [whose slogan is "Heal Your Life"] all over the world." Tanya also embraces spiritual teachings of gurus such as Wayne Dyer.

She says a spiritual teacher is "one who is able to embrace many religions, and often takes those best parts to share. I follow many of these teachers and meditation is a big part of my life, as is being part of nature." She cites the seven chakras, a Sanskrit word describing Eastern beliefs found in Hinduism, yoga, meditation, and other such spiritual sources, and strives to keep her own vibration level "high above my head, and going upward." She believes in auras and spiritual healing but says she is not gifted in those areas herself, adding, "I wish I could read your aura."

An aunt in a nursing home reported having visions as she approached death, and Tanya, though she herself has not had visions, believed her aunt. Tanya contends this was a part of her aunt's preparation for death and "the visions helped her to cross over. She lived for two years with one part of her failing body in this world and one, in the other."

One of Tanya's daughters works with her as a wedding officiant and is also an ordained reverend in the State of North Carolina. "While she is not as active in the business as I am, it's nice to be able to recommend her and to let her use my work," Tanya says. Her daughters sometimes attend spiritual conferences with her and the three maintain a close relationship.

Traditional ministers have had a mixed reaction to the wedding ministry as a business. "They didn't take us too seriously until about eight years ago when it exploded," Tanya says. Some of [the denominational ministers] perform as a way to make extra money, which is needed in the smaller churches." She relates a story about a traditional minister coming to her to learn about the business side of the wedding industry, seeking to supplement the small salary the congregation could pay. She says some ordained ministers in denominational churches are "coming around, realizing the financial gain" in a time when churches are struggling to pay salaries.

The OBX Wedding Association is "a kind of Better Business Bureau for weddings," says Tanya. Members pay a membership fee for a sort of "stamp of approval." The association holds a wedding show each year, prints a wedding magazine, and serves as a clearinghouse for couples seeking wedding planning assistance. Tanya is a member and believes the organization helps to maintain standards for the business part of the industry.

"It's all customer service and customer satisfaction in creating the perfect ceremony." Tanya receives many referrals for future work from couples she's married. Part of her duty as an officiant is returning the marriage license to the Register of Deeds office so the marriage can be legally recorded. She says, "I strive to conduct the perfect ceremony and return the license, which records the marriage."

Though marriages are the bulk of her work, she has performed other services as well. She has conducted memorials, often for family members of couples she's married, sometimes for elderly local residents. The hardest thing she's done was a memorial service for a child of a couple she'd previously married, when one of their three-year-old twins drowned in a swimming pool. She recalls, "Even in the worst of circumstances, which was the accidental death of a twin toddler whose parents I'd married, I never felt a spiritual bleakness—a heavy heart, yes, and a questioning of why. It was my inward spirituality that gave me the strength to do what needed to be done at this time and to comfort the family." She writes memorial and funeral services when asked to do so.

She has also christened babies of people she's married, sometimes using ocean water in a service on the beach at the same place where she'd married the couple previously. The christenings are very special to her. Tanya says a wedding, a christening, or a memorial service are "all a celebration of love, one fashion or another." For one local family, she's married three people, buried one, and christened a few.

When she performs a service, Tanya wears a robe designed for her by a theater costume designer—a white dress with a light coat that flows in the wind, making a "light, beachy, airy robe. Black doesn't work at the beach!"

Timing for an outdoor ceremony at the beach is tricky and becomes a practical matter of heat and light. Tanya has sometimes performed two ceremonies a day and her daughter, Rev. Tanya Barkley-Graham, may be performing another on a popular summer day. In summer, weddings are usually held between six and seven p.m., light enough for good photographs but after the strong heat of midday and when fewer people are on the beach. Part of Tanya's planning with the couple is helping them understand such realities of beach weddings. She says she performs marriage ceremonies all winter, but earlier in the day, sometimes in coats and heavy winter clothing.

Tanya conducts over fifty ceremonies annually. Recently she caught the ferry to Ocracoke, at the southernmost end of the Outer Banks, at one p.m., did the wedding at six-thirty p.m., and caught the ferry home, returning about midnight after a very long day. Alluding to her age, she says, "I can't do that anymore!"

In October 2014, North Carolina legalized same-sex marriage and Tanya remembers, "My phone began ringing immediately." She says, "I am an advocate of that community." Many of the calls were from people who had been together and committed for many years and wanted to formalize that commitment. "What an honor!" exclaims Tanya. She began writing ceremonies for these couples, changing the wording on her website to "couple," not "bride and groom," and using other inclusive language, adding pictures of same-sex couples. Her website says, "It is also my honor to perform same-sex marriages and I applaud this new legality in North Carolina."

She prepared herself for this expanded venture by going online and reading many websites, affiliating with same-sex sites. She feels "called upon to interpret as this day unfolds." She has learned that planning for same-sex marriages, while there was "an awful lot to learn," usually is about the same, with few distinctions from the traditional bride and groom. She advertises in a way that welcomes the LBGTQ (Lesbian, Bisexual, Gay, Transgender and Questioning) community. She laughs, "When I have to get witnesses, I get my good friends to witness and make sure they are inclusive."

The first same-sex couple she married were vacationing

here, after being committed to each other for twenty-two years. One of the partners was dying of cancer and had left the decision-making to her partner. She was in a wheelchair, and the registrar at the courthouse came out to the car for her to sign the necessary papers, demonstrating an attitude of openness that Tanya especially appreciated.

About one-third of Tanya's business the summer of 2015 was same-sex couples, more women than men, but male couples are beginning to book. She had wondered if men would want a woman officiating, but the four gay weddings booked so far have answered that question. She has seen weddings in the LBGTQ community grow from a couple with witnesses to full-fledged, well-attended events lately. Tanya anticipates that legalization of these ceremonies will have a significant impact on the wedding industry.

Tanya's website embodies her philosophy of wedding festivities. "Very often couples that seek our services are not comfortable with traditional church affiliation and desire a meaningful spiritual alternative … My goal as the writer is to create a ceremony that touches the hearts of you and your guests and speaks to your joined personality—an extension of you both." She recently gave a quote for a press release relating to the recent North Carolina law permitting same-sex marriage: "I certainly embrace this and feel if you have a public business, it should be available to all … As an ordained minister, I am honored to be available to all of the LGBTQ community."

Her advice to others interested in becoming ordained to do weddings is this: "Look at it as a business, not a hobby." She concludes her website with her personal belief: "I am passionate about creating a truly special ceremony that will become a treasured memory for you and your guests and embrace your wedding day as a joyful and defining moment which marks the beginning of your new life together."

However, she adds a coda in conversation. "I'm not the minister for everyone. If the party is more important, I'm not the minister for you. The ceremony should be a meaningful and memorable event for the couple."

CHAPTER 10
Gaye

GAYE MARSTON IS LEAD pastor of the Salem Fields Community Church, an affiliate of the Nazarene denomination.

"It's been a jagged journey," says Pastor Gaye, explaining how she came to be a pastor.

Salem Fields is one of the largest Nazarene congregations in the country, receiving about 1,100 worshippers on average each weekend. She and her husband, Buddy, also a lead pastor, manage a staff, a very large building complex, and the needs of their congregation, as well as a ministry in Port Harcourt, Nigeria. However, the way was not smooth nor the direction always obvious as she traversed her path.

She has not chosen to be ordained formally nor has she been to seminary, but she is fully supported by her denomination as lead pastor because of her strong educational and professional background, leadership capability, her years of service and personal religious experiences. She is also a licensed professional counselor and a licensed marriage and family therapist in Virginia.

Gaye is impassioned as she speaks, leaning forward with

direct eye contact and gesturing to emphasize her thoughts. At the age of sixty-two, she is trim and athletic-looking, with shoulder-length blonde hair, and wears dressy jeans, an embroidered green blouse and sandals. Her office is the meeting place for the interview with a soft couch and chair, and several windows that admit afternoon sunlight. A red electric bass guitar stands near the door and a peace pipe adorns the wall over a small desk.

As a child, Gaye was immersed in a religious family and a faith community, Mennonites, who were very active within their local church in Wauseon, OH, where she lived from age three to ten. As young as four years old, she accompanied her father to migrant communities where he preached and she and her cousin sang hymns. She recalls, "I loved that and that's where my heart for ministry began."

Born after three older brothers, the little girl became the proverbial apple of her father's eye. He was a carpenter and a leader in the church community. Her mother was a Methodist who was transformed into a Mennonite with the help of her new sisters-in-law, changing her clothing and hairstyle. The household was very traditional, with her mother minding the home, caring for her husband and children, while her father earned their living. A sister was born when Gaye was nine, bumping the siblings to five. She recalls her parents as having "hearts of love."

Gaye believes her Mennonite community exemplified "people loving people, relationships as priority and community gatherings as important. I got to experience a healthy body of Christ and received good solid Bible teaching." She sees these early years as critical in her faith development, though she later left the Mennonite denomination because of some of the legalistic rules for living.

The family moved to Virginia when Gaye was ten to be closer to her paternal grandparents. When she was fifteen, her father died suddenly, a devastating blow to the family. She was attending public school, a cheerleader and active in student government. "My mother went into a tailspin, into depression." Adding to the family's woe was the fact that her younger sister, only six years old, had discovered her father's body, causing the young child great emotional turmoil.

Gaye recalls, "Overnight life changed. We had to sell everything. My mother didn't know how to do finances or how to be a single parent. We sold our beautiful home, my horse, and said goodbye to our comfortable life, exchanging it for apartment living."

Gaye had her heart set on becoming an architect. "I loved math, watching my father read blueprints, the smell of lumber, and I was fascinated with the construction of buildings." She accompanied her father to jobs sometimes and dreamed of entering the architecture program at Virginia Tech. However, her father's death ended that dream.

Her mother took a job at Eastern Mennonite College, and Gaye had to leave her beloved high school and attend her senior year at Eastern Mennonite High School, still hoping to attend Virginia Tech. But because her mother's employment provided reduced tuition, it made Eastern Mennonite College (EMC, now Eastern Mennonite University in Harrisonburg, VA) her only option. "Mom provided the way to college, but I went to EMC kicking and screaming. I chose a physics major, unwilling to give up my hope of transferring to Virginia Tech School of Architecture. But by my sophomore year, I knew my dream had died. I began drifting. I think I gave up on my future."

She did transfer, to Temple University in a big city far away from the Mennonite lifestyle. "I was introduced to pot and alcohol and began to party." However, she kept "plugging away" and went back to Eastern Mennonite her senior year. Without much direction or passion and because she was somewhat gifted as an athlete, she defaulted with a degree in health and physical education. She had many courses in Christian education while she was a student there, which became her formal theological training.

After graduating with her physical education degree, though she was qualified to teach school, she got a job as assistant manager of sporting goods at a newly opened K-Mart. She moved into a house with her mother in Keezelton, VA, and her little sister became friends with the sister of Gaye's later-to-be-husband. "I was a party girl and wanted to be in control of my own life. Buddy and I met and our relationship was based simply on having fun and no commitment. We dated for a year and got engaged. During that time I took a trip to England and Scotland for my brother's wedding, and that began my lifelong love of travel."

When their engagement was announced, Gaye's mother worried that her intended husband was not a Christian. Not having her approval, the young people eloped. The day after the ceremony, Gaye thought, "Dear God, what have I done? I cried and cried. But when I came around, I decided I'd made a vow to God and couldn't find a loophole to get out. I realized I needed to suck it up and make this thing [marriage] happen." Forty years later, they are still married and pastor their church together.

She quit work, and a year and a half later their daughter, their only child, was born. Gaye remembers that a few years later, "I became pretty convicted about not living the party lifestyle. I wanted my daughter to have better. Mom gave me good advice: 'Go back to church.' My husband had become very possessive of me, so he agreed to go to church with me so other guys wouldn't hit on me." After exploring Mennonite churches, they were invited to a Nazarene church.

She began researching what the Bible says about various topics, especially about marriage and God's view of war. "I'd been taught a lot of good but a lot of folklore, too, and I needed to discover and develop a personal faith and belief. I was doing a lot of questioning and learning," she says.

Gaye believes this time of uncertainty serves her well now as pastor. She sees questioning as a healthy part of faith development and believes her role is to "walk alongside people as they discover what truth God reveals to them in a relationship with Christ."

Becoming a minister was not part of her life plan. After finding a new church home, however, she quickly became involved leading the youth ministry. Buddy assisted her as she led retreats, a traveling musical group and weekly youth services.

Gaye continued her graduation education in counseling. After earning her master of education degree at James Madison University (JMU), she wanted to continue in the educational specialist degree program and become licensed as a therapist. Her motivation was evident as she had high test scores and grade point average and had recently attended a conference held by the American Association of Christian Counselors. During the interview at JMU, she talked about her aspirations to become a Christian counselor, and she speculates that emphasis may have contributed to not being accepted into the advanced program.

With no further options in Harrisonburg to advance her education, a door opened when a church in northern Virginia, Woodbridge Church of the Nazarene, called both Gaye and her husband to serve on staff. He became a youth pastor and she, a professional counselor. Having a professional counselor on the staff of a church was innovative at that time.

Gaye applied to George Mason University and was accepted into the advanced postgraduate program in counseling. She earned her counseling licenses, developed a counseling center, and still maintains a small private practice, though "not with my own parishioners," she's quick to add.

Gaye and her husband moved to Fredericksburg twenty years ago to share the pastorate of a small Nazarene church, a call she says they "accepted out of obedience. We were personally ready to get out of full-time ministry, but we sensed the Lord wanted us to do this."

She says, "The Nazarenes, a holiness tradition based on the theology of John Wesley, are very accepting of women but still very patriarchal. In reality, it has been painful in the man-world at this level of leadership. I never wanted to make an issue. I was raised not to and value being respectful in the midst of injustice. But God called me, whether it's easy or not, and I had to continue to pursue His path for my life. I've been able to make great progress in establishing a new paradigm for leadership."

Initially the congregation, "and even I, unknowingly, all looked at my husband as the lead pastor because of an unspoken traditional mindset of the man as pastor. But there came a time when I realized God had used me as much as my husband. It was then I began to have to speak up. It was a painful process to learn to speak up."

Regarding the pastorate, she says, "I never set out to be to be one! But I realized this is where God led me, so I've served in obedience and with all my heart. I've been a pioneer but I never chose that." She says it has naturally caused some problems in her marriage, which has had to change and grow by course-correcting their roles.

When she heard someone in her congregation refer to her as

the "pastor's wife" and realized even her husband didn't acknowledge her contribution, "It started my thinking to a whole new place. I said, wait a minute! That's where the realization of injustice emerged. I didn't know what to do with it, so it drove me to my knees. God and I began chipping away, plowing the ground. I could give it up and skip the pain or be obedient to God and stand up for myself. It's been brutal and at great personal cost. I entered with a traditional mindset on marriage and ministry and it got in the way. We are now co-pastors, equally called and acknowledged and responsible to fulfill that call to the best of our ability. I've had to work at that, I've had to push."

She says her leadership has "always been a work in progress. I want to be respectful but push the envelope. I stay close to Jesus. I keep my eyes on Jesus."

About five years ago she decided to seek counseling for herself. In what she calls a God-moment, she began conversing with a woman she was seated next to on an international flight from Nigeria. The woman gave her the name of a counselor that Gaye believes has done her much good in sorting out her thoughts and feelings. "Over my life, I had learned to deny my feelings and that was detrimental. I studied what Jesus meant by turning the other cheek and the difference from enabling. I put scripture and counseling together. I sought what the church hasn't taught beyond simply forgiving. I allowed my fears to come out and recovered my anger.

"I stayed close to Jesus, studied His mind. I became a fighter. I would say most of my adult life I've spent protecting the church and my husband, at the expense of me. That's not what Christ called us to do so I had to find the error of my thinking and theology. I regret not seeking help sooner. It helped me so much." She's now working on a book, *What Jesus Meant by Turning the Other Cheek*.

Of her own ministry, she says, "All my adult life, in the heat of any turmoil I've chosen to turn to God instead of other avenues like divorce, substances or running away. Success to me has meant that my children [daughter, son-in-law and grandchildren] are still choosing to live by faith in Jesus Christ. I can't look back and say anything is a mistake. I feel grateful that God has used me, even as I've stumbled along the way."

However, she laments that she'd love for people to comment more on the message she delivers about Christ, rather than on "having a good hair day or judging my clothes or seeing me as a woman. I'm a person first. It took me a long time to make peace with all the stereotypes. I even had to learn that my height was intimidating to some." But she says she can now get beyond them because "I have an understanding that I'm in a different place."

Her advice to a young woman contemplating entering the ministry is, "Embrace the obstacles as part of the process instead of fighting them as impediments. I would say, if it's an obstacle, it's part of who God is growing you to be."

Their church, Salem Fields Community Church, is an outgrowth of the little congregation they came to pastor twenty years ago. They outgrew their building and "God gave us a vision. We knew we needed a new facility." Some land became available but their congregation numbered only about sixty-five people.

"We said, yeah, right," believing they could not find the money for the purchase. They raised $300,000 and secured the land only one day before a major development was announced right across the street. She says, "They'd quoted us a price and had to sell it to us. It was a miracle. We got seventy-seven acres, now valued at $12 million." They sold a few parcels of their land and gradually built their church in phases.

The modern complex includes a large auditorium, several hallways of classrooms, offices, and a large, welcoming open space, surrounded by a vast parking lot. An attractive cafe in the lobby sells various coffees, breakfast pastries, and heartier lunch fare such as barbecue. A pre-K learning center cares for up to two hundred children daily. The facility gets heavy use from the secular community, from after-prom parties to food bank annual meetings, weddings, Wounded Warrior gatherings and much more. "We give our building away. We want to be a good partner serving with our community," Gaye says.

"We're a friendly, come-as-you-are, no church-face kind of place, even though we have the dynamic of a large group with maybe 1,100 people on a weekend." Her daughter is worship director and her son-in-law, missions pastor. She says her daughter has a beautiful voice and Gaye sometimes plays bass guitar during worship services, laughing as she says that satisfies her creative side.

She says the church has a relaxed atmosphere to attract people. The pastors try to see their ministry "from the point of view of people not attending, those turned off to church or never knowing Jesus." In the past they've had motorcycle rallies for church services and they treat the surrounding area to a fine fireworks display on Labor Day. As one of the biggest Nazarene congregations in the country, "God has honored us," Gaye says.

A painful part of her life has been people leaving without saying goodbye, both in her family and in the church. All her brothers were divorced and she had to grieve the loss of their wives and children. At this point all her siblings but one have passed on, as have her parents and others in her family. She and her remaining brother travel once a year on what they call "no regrets trips." Just the two of them have been to Hawaii,

Ireland, Israel and Iceland. She says, "It has been a beautiful way to reconcile losses of family and celebrate what we have left." She loves to travel and takes her grandchildren on various travel adventures, also.

"My taillights are brighter than my headlights," she says. "Looking back I can see how things have transpired and worked together, more so than being able to see the future. But I do know Who holds my future and I trust Him. I try to be grateful for the jagged path I've taken, even the drifting. But I wonder about it sometimes. My plans were a bit off. I wanted to be an architect of buildings, but God has led me to be an architect of souls. I'm grateful for that."

At this point in her life, looking to her future, she says, "God hasn't released us from Salem Fields Community Church yet, so I'll do what I know to do in this journey of faith. I'll obediently take whatever next step He shows me, pursue God and never give up on His faithfulness."

CHAPTER 11
Jann

JANET ANN (JANN) BRISCOE is parish associate at the St. Simons (GA) Presbyterian Church and an ordained minister in the Presbyterian Church USA.

When she said she was going into the ministry, Jann's father said, "I had always wanted you to be a lawyer but maybe we need a minister more." She recalls, "That was an affirmation, so important, such a gift." Today, more than three decades later, she still feels her ministry is a gift in her life.

Jann has impressive academic credentials. She earned a bachelor's degree in psychology from Vanderbilt University and completed education courses at then Peabody College (now a part of Vanderbilt University). The following year she earned a master's degree in special education from Georgia State University. Other academic work includes a master of divinity from Columbia Seminary in Decatur, GA, an educational specialist degree in counseling from the University of North Carolina-Greensboro, and doctoral level work in pastoral theology at Princeton Seminary.

As part-time parish associate in a large Presbyterian church, she directs the Stephen Ministry program, works in pastoral care and does other assorted work, "a lot of 'assorted,'" she adds with a laugh. Stephen Ministry is a non-denominational ministry named for St. Stephen, who was appointed a deacon by the apostles to distribute food and other aid to poor people in the early church. Stephen Ministry today is a lay Christian caring program that supplements pastoral care by providing weekly one-on-one accompaniment for persons in challenging situations.

The church Jann serves is committed to its outreach programs, especially the hunger action team, summer mission trips for youth, adults and their families, and hospitality to Alcoholics Anonymous groups. Jann is also a licensed professional counselor and maintains a small private practice in marriage and family counseling, most of which is pro bono work. She is married to a retired Presbyterian minister who is also a clinical social worker.

Jann is a child of south Georgia, though she left the state to attend a boarding school in Fort Lauderdale for her high school years. Her family provided her with strong religious ties. Her maternal grandmother was a charter member of the Blackshear Presbyterian Church in Blackshear, GA, and her grandfather was Sunday School superintendent for fifty years at that church. Both died before she was born but she feels their legacy when she preaches at that church, as she currently does the first Sunday of each month. She was very active in the church growing up, attending Sunday School and youth group and teaching vacation Bible school classes while she was a young teenager. She describes herself as "kind of absent from church" during her later high school and college years.

After graduating from Vanderbilt, she taught students with learning disabilities for four years but she knew she didn't want to continue in that field. She endured some distressing years about that time as her first marriage ended and her mother died. These two events of loss happened in close proximity, and she entered a very difficult time in her life. She thought she'd go to graduate school in either psychology or counseling, but those plans didn't work out. She applied to several schools and was not admitted or was wait-listed for some schools she wanted to attend, though she was admitted to one she didn't relish attending.

About that time she was on the search committee for a new minister for her church. She helped the family move in and settle into the community and became friends with them during that process. The new minister asked her if she'd ever thought about being a minister, and she remembers saying, "Kind of, maybe."

She really wanted to attend graduate school at Georgia State University and traveled to Atlanta, intending to talk to them about how to bolster her application. She was heading home and thought about her earlier conversation with her pastor about entering the ministry. She called to talk with him and learned he was coming to Atlanta the next day. He offered to meet her at the seminary (Columbia Seminary in Decatur, a suburb of Atlanta) the next morning. At the time Jann was living with her father, so she asked the pastor to let him know she'd be staying with cousins in Atlanta instead of coming home that night. She recalls her pastor saying, "I'll tell your dad you're staying over but not what you're doing in the morning. You do that."

Jann met her pastor at the seminary, had an interview, filled out an application, and "it was like all the balls on the pool table moved together to go into the right pockets." Everything fell into place and she enrolled in summer school to begin work on her second master's degree, this time in divinity.

Although there were other women who were her classmates at Columbia Seminary, at that time, Jann knew no other female ministers, though she did know that some women were missionaries. At Columbia Seminary she was in the second wave of women students "so a good bit of the initial groundbreaking had already been done four or five years prior." She became the first female candidate for ministry in the Savannah Presbytery, a regional administrative arm of the Presbyterian Church USA serving southeastern Georgia, currently comprising forty-three congregations.

After seminary Jann accepted a call to be associate pastor at John Calvin Presbyterian Church in Metairie, LA, where she served for three years. She then went to Princeton University where she worked on doctoral studies while holding part-time jobs as interim hospital chaplain, a hospice chaplain, and pastoral coordinator at a Disciples of Christ (DCC) church in Levittown, PA. She recalls the time at the DCC church especially fondly, saying she really appreciated their adherence to the credo, "We are Christians only, not the only Christians." She liked the weekly communion service and the prominent role of the laity in that denomination.

Jann moved to North Carolina and "was supposed to be working on my dissertation, but it just wasn't to be." She was hired as spiritual care coordinator in a Winston-Salem hospice and finally decided not to continue with her dissertation. She wrote to her advisor and resigned from the program "but grieved that decision for years." She said only about five years ago was she able to "put that one to rest."

Early in her move to North Carolina, she began to do supply preaching in the Salem Presbytery, becoming many congregations' first experience with a clergywoman. "I enjoyed it. Often I was the first experience of a woman minister. One woman said to me, 'Oh, I could actually hear you!', making me wonder what she expected—a soft-spoken sermon?" She remembers that some members of congregations would shake her hand but didn't meet her eye as they exited the church.

Jann believes experiences of clergymen and clergywomen are relatively equal in her denomination as a whole, though there are areas where this is not true. Guidelines for clergy salaries from the Presbytery and Synod protect women from salary discrimination to some degree in the Presbyterian Church USA. However, one female clergy friend of hers in another state was told she needed to lower her financial expectations when she applied for a solo pastor's position after having been an associate pastor for many years. The perception seemed to be that she was entry level again. As in other denominations, Presbyterian women sometimes accept jobs in smaller congregations that can't afford a full-time minister.

The joys of Jann's ministry seem to center around pastoral care. She recalls visiting a woman who'd had a miscarriage who was "blown away that I was there to acknowledge her loss." She enjoys participating in the liturgy, especially of special services. She sees leading worship as a very creative process and enjoys preaching once a month at the church where she grew up in Blackshear, though the church has changed since she was a child. The church "has been through struggles" and Jann was a participant in addressing those by serving on an administrative commission sent by the Presbytery. She enjoys serving in that church, including the occasional pastoral care she does there, and feels well received: "I am theirs."

Her own response to pastoral work has changed over the years. Some of the same underlying motivation that led her to clergy life motivates her study and practice of psychology, counseling, and ministry. She is "interested in helping, supporting individuals to grow and change. It's a pleasure to meet persons, hear their stories, make a connection with their life and faith journey."

She adds, "I've come to appreciate that I am a natural teacher," following in the steps of her mother, who was a teacher. Her father was also a school principal for a few years before he entered his wife's family's business. Perhaps her greatest joy is "being present at significant moments" of her parishioners.

One incident she recalls happened when she was an associate pastor. She asked, "If Bob [the senior minister] gets to go to Women of the Church luncheons, do I get to go to the Men of the Church breakfast?" After some hesitation and thought, the group invited her. "So I went, and they asked the 'honorary man' to pray," she says, laughing.

About four years ago Jann began receiving spiritual direction from an older woman in her congregation who is a trained classical spiritual director and she has found that to be transforming. She embarked on a personal spiritual growth experience sponsored by the Shalem Institute for Spiritual Formation, an ecumenical organization dedicated to spiritual growth. The website describes the organization: "The Shalem Institute provides in-depth support for contemplative living and leadership—a way of being in the world that is prayerfully attentive and responsive to God's presence and guidance."

She joined the sixteen-month program on spiritual growth and leadership for clergy. The program involves a lot of work at home, extended reading and reflection, and two week-long residencies at a retreat center in Maryland. She finds the program to be inspirational and she feels very "cared for and humbled. That's my calling currently."

Jann says, "There I came to learn about and experience

contemplative theology and spirituality. I recognized contemplative theology and spirituality as the home I had always known at some level. Shalem introduced me to this ancient tradition and provided me with language to express what my soul knew. It more and more shapes how I understand myself, the church, how I see other people, how I see the world."

Another important influence in her spiritual development has been an annual conference for progressive Christians on the emerging church, held at Epworth by the Sea, a Christian retreat center on St. Simons owned by the United Methodist Church. At the annual "January Adventure" conference, she has heard outstanding religious leaders and read writings from such influential Christian authors as Marcus Borg, Jon Dominic Crossan, Barbara Brown Taylor, Richard Rohr, Walter Brueggemann, Nadia Bolz-Weber, and Brian McClaren. She terms it a "gathering to educate, support and encourage progressive Christians" and it has been influential in her current spiritual thinking.

Jann has become an advocate of the teaching of theologians such as Thomas Merton, Thomas Keating and Richard Rohr on the true-self and false-self. Rohr introduced the concept of first and second halves of life, where the first half is focused on constructing a container that can hold the content that is the focus of the second half of life. In the last ten or fifteen years Jann has been increasingly intentional in her practice of contemplative spiritual disciplines as the foundation for her personal and professional life.

She often feels frustration with "the church as an institution." She sees and believes "how much more the church is called to be, can be, and we settle for so much less." She recounts sitting through staff meetings talking about details of programs, with the evaluation often being "how many people can it attract?"

She believes in raising the questions, "Why are we offering this program, what is its purpose? How does it contribute to faith development and spiritual growth?" Regarding youth programs, she believes we have "a tendency, a temptation, to lower our expectations to meet what we think members will support rather than doing something that challenges them."

She says we are "better at developing good church members than making, empowering disciples. It is more important to Jesus to follow Him than to speak right words about Him." She hopes "the church will provide opportunities and experiences that encourage persons at all stages of spiritual/faith development to grow throughout their lives. Success cannot always be measured in numbers." She believes that summarizes the mission of contemplative practices for churches, to change peoples' consciousness and "remove either-or thinking."

It is hard for Jann to imagine what her life would have been like if she hadn't become a clergywoman. Her realization of her calling came at the very dark time in her life after she'd suffered losses of her mother and her marriage. She read a book of prayers by Michael Quoist over and over during this time. The format was some scripture followed by a written prayer, then a response formatted in what might be God's voice. One prayer was about darkness, the only one in the book without an answering response, she recalls. Jann relates, "I read it every night for awhile and cried myself to sleep. Eventually the message came clear that if I wanted to be part of the healing and growth of people, I could not do that apart from God."

She's not sure to this day if choosing to do a program in counseling moved her away from ministry or became an adjunct to that calling. Over the years, she'd had troubled feelings, almost a visceral reaction, to the term Christian counselor. She believes she represents a different blend of ministering and counseling and now sees the merit in the combination of the two as she works with people who identify as Christians and want to change their lives.

"My lens is faith and spiritual questions." She laughs and says she never expected to be on the staff of a large church since most of her experience has been in small churches. She serves a predominantly upper-middle-class congregation on one of the beautiful barrier islands off the Georgia coast, somewhat surprised that she ended up there. She says "I asked God, 'What are You up to?'" and received the reply that she's right where God wants her to be.

A ministry of particular interest to Jann at the moment is Savannah Presbytery's commitment to the development of an alternative worshipping community, a missional church in an interfaith community for worship and service to reach out to the marginalized in society by providing payment for a half-time call for this purpose. The idea is that non-denominational worship will occur not in a traditional way but rather at other times during the week than Sunday morning and people may still retain membership in their own churches if they wish. Jann is on the leadership team for that initiative.

She has come to believe through her contemplative study that "God is always with us, is the spirit within us. God is always present." She believes that some prayers, including those of some pastors, do not reflect this belief and says, "I can't pray that way anymore." She gave the example of saying, for example, if a person is sick, not "God, be with John" but rather, "May John know that God is with him."

Jann's advice to women contemplating the ministry would be to "give priority to your own spiritual life. Schedule it on the calendar if necessary and then share that information with the Session [governing board of the church]. Do things that call to mind, enable you to revisit your sense of calling. Find a person or group that will support you in holding you to the priorities you've set."

Jann says jokingly, "God called me to the ministry to ensure I'd be in church on Sunday. There's probably some truth in that ..." Clearly her time on Sundays and throughout the week, in church and out of church, is given freely as she seeks to follow where the Spirit leads, sharing love and joy and hope.

CHAPTER 12
Margaret

MARGARET SEQUEIRA OF RICHMOND, VA, is a consulting minister for the Unitarian-Universalist Church.

"Take a leap of faith but look over the edge to see how deep the cliff you're diving off of is," Margaret Sequeira advises anyone who is contemplating entering the ministerial life. She traces her path as logical and thoughtful, but it has included some economic realities she believes women should know about before they enter the profession of ministry.

Margaret came from a religious Roman Catholic family, "a post-Vatican II child" who knew the church in its "moment of opening" as it transformed itself into a denomination more responsive to the world's concerns. She attended Catholic school growing up in California, taught by nuns. Her family was always active in church, with her father ordained as a deacon after Margaret graduated from college. Her mother teaches religion in an all-girls school and also attended seminary, though Margaret says it was hard for her father to accept the idea of her mother as a seminarian.

She credits them as being inspirational for her: "I followed their example," saying pastoral care was always important in their family and her parents were leaders in their church. She grew up raising questions, to which her father would answer, "Margaret, church is not a democracy." She says, "It would never dawn on him there was another way [other than the Roman Catholic way] to organize a church."

Questioning was a crucial part of Margaret's faith development. She had issues with the papacy and the curia. She says, "I saw the leaders of the Roman Catholic Church as a small group out of touch with the Church in general." She feels very fortunate to be guided by people throughout her years of study who encouraged her questions.

Margaret followed her childhood tradition on to Catholic colleges. She earned her bachelor's degree from Georgetown University in history with a minor in theology, and a master's in theological studies in ethics and social theory from the Jesuit School of Theology at Santa Clara University at Berkeley. She also took courses at Wesley Theological Seminary in Washington, DC, a Methodist seminary that welcomes people from other denominations. Later she attended Starr King School for Ministry in Berkeley for a year of Unitarian Universalist education. She formally entered the ordination process in that denomination in 2007 and is currently in the process of ordination.

She was very active in campus ministry when she attended Georgetown, choosing that school in part because she wanted to attend college in the East. She took the introduction to Catholic theology course from Professor Monika Hellwig and was introduced to feminist Catholic theology for the first time. Hellwig was a former religious sister who had left her community for an academic career at Georgetown after attaining a law degree from the University of Liverpool and a doctorate from Catholic University. Hellwig was later president / executive director of the Association of Catholic Colleges and Universities and earlier in her career had been one of the few women with ready access to the Vatican as a research assistant there.

Margaret recalls that Hellwig was a big influence on her thinking: "For the first time I got to look at history and the 'why' of belief and practice. This opened a whole series of questions about women's role in the church."

She began questioning whether she could continue with integrity in the Roman Catholic tradition. Her spiritual director, a Jesuit, told her to take a break and step back. "I gave up the Church for Lent," she says with a laugh. "I wasn't ready to give up all I knew. They [her spiritual directors and professors] didn't shut down my questions. I was told questions are welcome, explore them. That's always a gift, very validating. I was very blessed in my life and received support for the journey, my questions. How can I now pay it forward, say to others, your questions are okay, important, don't hold them back?"

After graduating from Georgetown, Margaret moved home to California to figure out what to do next as she embarked on a series of jobs in various religious communities. She became a liaison between thirty-three parishes and Catholic Charities. She connected the charities and congregations, packed holiday baskets, and provided education in the schools on poverty and homeless. She educated youth on how people descended into poverty by having kids create their own budgets to see how finances work. During this time she volunteered with the church and actually joined a different parish than where her parents were, to create her own identity. She recalls that she was really struggling with whether or not she could stay within the Roman Catholic faith. She wasn't willing to lie or to be silent about her doubts and distrust of the Church hierarchy.

Next she tried the Episcopal church after deciding she would leave both the Roman Catholic church and California. She moved back to the Washington area with friends and got involved at the National Cathedral. "I threw myself into being Episcopalian."

Her parish rector was a woman and she witnessed the ordination of Jane Dixon as the first woman Episcopal bishop. "I felt the wonder of being a little Roman Catholic girl watching women become bishops." She saw women with significant clergy roles for the first time. She also worked at St. Albans Episcopal School in Washington.

Holding various jobs, Margaret searched for her career while she was Episcopalian. She wanted to go to graduate school but wasn't sure what she wanted to study. She was wait-listed for law school. She didn't feel called to ordination but wanted to study theology. She was interested in ethics and religion in society, still dominant interests for her today. She began questioning key doctrines of Christianity, including the divinity of Christ. She attended the John Wesley Seminary and became acquainted with several Unitarian Universalist students there. She was not seeking ordination, but simply wanted to study and learn more.

Margaret's partner, Donna, was in technology, so they moved back to California. She sometimes "kicks myself" because with only one more more year, she'd have had a degree if she'd stayed in school at that time. It became clear to her that she wanted a child, so she worked to reduce their family debt so they could start a family.

They had a daughter and agreed they'd raise her in a religious community, so they went "church-shopping." At that time, the 1990s, many mainline denominations were studying the issue of gay and lesbian inclusion in churches. Episcopalians and Lutherans were quietly ordaining gays and lesbians. Margaret says, "My partner and I were not willing to live in a closet." At that time, she believed, too many seminaries would have kicked her out if she were open. This had a big impact on what church they attended. "We did not want to make a liberal statement, just be a part of a community." They affiliated with the Unitarian Universalists (UU) in 1999.

Both Margaret and Donna were active in the UU church. After the California boom and bust of technology, both took jobs at Stanford. Margaret wanted to study ethics and religion. At one time she was enrolled in two schools simultaneously and held two part-time jobs—"It was a crazy time"—and worked in religious education at the UU church. She did administrative tasks and a lot of teacher training and work with parents. She became involved in leading worship and did some preaching in the UU church.

It was too expensive to stay in school, so Margaret took a job as a full-time director of lifespan development at the UU church in Williamsburg, VA. She was their first full-time staff member, directing everything from nursery through adult education. She taught and did campus ministry. "I gave young adults the opportunity to learn and question, paying back my Georgetown experience at William and Mary."

The past year has been a transition for Margaret. She has been a guest preacher and then she took a half-time job as consulting minister in Kitty Hawk, NC, where she, her spouse, and their daughter live. She had wanted a full-time job but was unable to find one so "I cobbled some things together," she says, and has been employed as a half-time clergywoman for the past year and a half.

The joys of congregational leadership for Margaret have included "creating and leading worship in collaboration with other people, a very creative experience." She loves the congregational tradition of UU churches, with their dislike of doctrine of the trinity. She cites history, including the king of Transylvania, who was Unitarian, and Universalists in Europe, especially England. She says, "The fights are a little different in congregational churches such as the UU denomination where the emphasis is on congregational polity, outliers, the goodness of humanity, and the view that God's love is inclusive enough for everyone to be saved."

One of Margaret's memorable pastoral experiences is sitting with a dying ninety-three-year-old woman and reading poetry to her. "What an honor. As a minister you witness this [transition to death], but it's hard."

While congregational involvement can bring real joy to the pastor, it also has an unstable, volatile aspect to it. She says, "The pastor and congregation have a weird relationship. On the one hand, you are the leader of the church. Yet your salary, etc., go back to the board. You have to be careful how unpopular you are. There are lots of congregational concerns and that's not my passion." She explains, "I am more interested in what new ways community comes together and answering questions." However, she acknowledges, "Many are so in love with congregational life. That's the minister you choose to be your leader."

Another concern of being a minister is, she says, "Being a leader of a congregation takes a person's spirituality and makes it public. It's a real gift to lead a congregation, but a minister also has to feed herself spiritually." That can be hard, especially when the nearest colleague may be a few hours away if the congregation is in a more rural area, as has been the case for Margaret lately.

"You can lose why you were a member of a congregation, and

that makes it hard. It can be a challenge if you want to experience more broadly, other related paths. It can be hard to find places okay to do that. You have a responsibility to your own community and you lose some freedom. That's balanced against the privilege of preaching. It's an amazing gift to be able to do that."

The Unitarian tradition historically included the Transcendentalists—Ralph Waldo Emerson, Margaret Fuller, and Henry David Thoreau—and others with a humanist bent. Margaret says, "Some have called it a church without God, a big theology tent." She explains that many people come from other denominations. The UU church welcomes women as well as men, questioners, gays and lesbians. Church members have been active in civil rights, from early abolitionists to marching in Selma.

Margaret says the UU is known for open theology, embracing everyone from those who strongly believe in God, liberal Christians, Jews, to even a contingent of pagans. "The denomination practices very broad theology, including people deeply wrestling with religion and Christianity, being as open as possible to questions." She explains it's hard to pin down exactly what a group is, what themes, who are you talking about, emphasizing capturing people's experience.

Margaret believes self-care is really important for ministers. "We all struggle with how to do it, keep a Sabbath, how not to have a twenty-four/seven job. ... You need a way you can turn it off. It's hard to turn it off when you're the minister."

She says, "Religion today is becoming less true, sometimes anti-God," with some polarization but also with openness to ideas. Religion has shifted as younger generations show more openness to diversity of language, bringing their own kind of curiosity. Margaret says, "Women's traditional rituals have their own gifts, lighting the chalice, water from summer, flower communion."

The UU church was among the first to ordain women. Over half of their ministers today are women. There are no formal barriers in the denomination, Margaret says, but there's still an old boys' network, though no actual roadblock.

Her advice to women contemplating ministry is, "Get as clear as you can what your vocation is, what you're being called to, whether or not ministry is the best way to live out your call. The clearer you are, the more discernment. It's a huge commitment, a lot of years, a lot of money. The clearer you are, the better, no rose-colored glasses."

She continues, "Know the process in your denomination. Learn as much as possible, check for hidden roadblocks. Don't leave women out of the conversation. Women are trained not to do that, not to ask questions. There has to be a cost-benefit analysis of jobs and how well they will pay. Don't be afraid to ask for what you're worth. Pay is sometimes frozen and stagnated. Can you work without higher pay, no job benefits? It will affect your ministry if you can't."

Her strongest advice is, "Money is important. Don't ignore it and don't pretend it's not important." She says, "There's a tension in all religious communities now. Women will be asked, 'Isn't this your call? Aren't you doing this for God?'" adding, "God doesn't pay the rent!"

At this point in her life, Margaret is looking for her next career steps. "I want to step back and see how much I want my job, what life might look life more blended, where you'd go home and you're done for the day with your job." She is currently providing full financial support for her family. "My family needs me to support them and I can't support my family with ministry."

Margaret and Donna homeschool their high-school-aged daughter, with her spouse taking the lead role in that. Margaret says the decision to homeschool has been a good one. Since they have moved from California to Virginia to North Carolina, along with the non-traditional circumstance of being a two-mom family, the continuity of homeschooling has been advantageous to their daughter. "She is academically gifted and a real joy to us."

At this point in her life Margaret doesn't plan to go back to full-time congregational ministry. She says, "I am very blessed by my congregational experience, especially since I haven't done all the hoops [for ordination]." She explains that ministerial jobs are becoming fewer and they don't pay very well, particularly in religious education.

Margaret and her family will move back to Virginia soon for her to seek full-time employment, perhaps teaching or other academic work. She will continue to do some formal ministry of a freelance variety, weddings and funerals, for the many people who do not affiliate with a church, saying, "Preaching is a form of teaching." She also plans to do workshops and writing. She believes that ministry is but one of many rewarding paths and that people don't have to be limited to one vision. "I'll keep my hand in but do it my own way. The gift of now is that is a possibility."

She reminds us, "Overall, the exciting thing about where we are is both so much unknown possibility of where we're going. The faith community will have to adapt."

"Scattered Revelations," Margaret's blog, will show us where her next path is leading her.

CHAPTER 13

Kate

KATE COSTA, THIRTY-ONE, IS pastor of St. Luke's Lutheran Church (ELCA) in Culpeper, VA.

"I feel often I stand on the shoulders of giants," says Kate, paraphrasing a quote from Isaac Newton often attributed to Nelson Mandela. She is in a line of both female and male Lutheran pastors, just as Newton was in physics and Mandela in human rights.

Kate, ordained at the age of twenty-seven, has been at St. Luke's Lutheran Church in Culpeper for four and a half years. Tall and slim, she is professionally dressed in a gray knee-length skirt with a faint chalk-stripe pattern, a black blouse with a pristine clerical collar, and a maroon tapestry-weave cotton jacket. Black ballerina flats and small silver earrings complete the outfit, along with sunglasses atop her hair. She looks just what she is, ready for anything. She can call on a parishioner at the hospital, give a blessing, negotiate a contract for use of her building, offer a prayer at a community event, mop up a spilled soft drink in the church kitchen, or burp a baby in this outfit.

A cradle Lutheran, Kate grew up in Abingdon, VA, at St. John

Lutheran Church. She and her family—she has two brothers and two sisters, all younger—were always active in church, "always the last ones to leave." Her mother sang in the choir and her father taught Sunday school and served on the Church Council, the governing board of St. John.

Kate's family traces their Lutheran heritage through a great-grandfather, a brew-master in Germany who emigrated to Wisconsin in 1849. Her maternal grandfather was an organist in a Lutheran church who moved his family to Colorado. Kate's father, a lawyer, as a young man decided to drive across country in a Volkswagen van and met his future wife, Kate's mother, in Colorado on that trip. Several of her family members have been adopted from Asia. She says, "Our family has been willing to take the joyous leap of adoption across generations. My mother is also adopted, and we consider it a wonderful way to form a family."

When she enrolled at the College of William and Mary, Kate thought she would become a doctor. She initially studied biology, then was drawn to social science and achieved a bachelor's degree in neuroscience, a hybrid of biology and psychology. She discovered she was more interested in people than in science alone.

She really enjoyed her work as a camp counselor at Caroline Furnace Lutheran Camp at Fort Valley, VA, in the Massanutten Mountains as a summer job. She did other volunteer church jobs and at some point realized that all the things she chose to do in her spare time were "related to the Gospel. I always chose working for the church." She decided perhaps her interests lay not so much in medicine as in working with the church. Kate says she was a good student but the academic work did not come easily to her. She found her religion classes the easiest and ultimately the most compelling part of her undergraduate curriculum.

Realizing "my free time could be full time," she decided to pursue a religious vocation.

She graduated with honors and a master's degree from the Lutheran Theological Seminary in Philadelphia in 2011. She chose that seminary, one of eight ELCA seminaries in the U.S., because she felt they understood the role of science in theology. Given her own scientific undergraduate training, that was important to her. For example, she wanted to know "how to reconcile teachings about creation and evolution, not have them swept under the rug."

Her program of preparation included a year working as a pastoral intern with the American Church in Berlin (ACB). She felt well accepted as a woman working in the church in Germany, which also has a history of ordaining women to the ministry. According to Wikipedia, the ACB is an ecumenical and international congregation that was established in the 19th century. ACB's members come from more than seventeen Christian denominations and from more than thirty different nations. The congregation is loosely affiliated with the Evangelical Lutheran Church in America, from which the congregation receives clergy support. The ACB offers services in English and is involved in social action outreach, such as feeding programs, in Berlin.

"This program is called *Laib und Selle* (Bread and Soul) and was one of my favorite parts of working in Berlin," Kate recalls. "Each Friday we would move the pews forward to make room for tables of vegetables and day-old bread. There the women would teach me the German words for produce, and I in turn shared bread with our neighbors in need."

The internship assignment in Berlin was one of the few times she has experienced difficulty because she is a woman. Earlier she had asked her seminary advisors for an internship with a clergywoman as a mentor. She had never had a woman pastor growing up, though she always knew they existed. As a child she had heard an Episcopal female deacon read the Gospel and thought that was really inspiring.

Her internship advisors not only agreed with her, but also were not sure she should do the ACB internship in Berlin because there was no clergywoman to serve as her mentor. Kate found herself arguing with her advisory group against the request she herself had already made, almost finding her words used against her, as she realized the "global development was more important." Though she realizes women must support each other, a far stronger value for her is that people, both men and women, should support each other. She has strong collegial ties with pastors of both genders.

She also served as an intern at a mission church in Fredericksburg, VA, a church that did not take root. She says, "As a woman, it was easier for me to knock on a door and invite someone to church, less intimidating for them." However, she believes women can be stereotyped as being nurturing caregivers and not seen as having the background to do anything but pastoral care, youth and family work.

"Some people just don't want a woman running the business of the church. That attitude needs to change, for the sake of women and also men. While there may be no overt difference, covert differences may not make things equal." Overall, however, Kate has been "pleasantly surprised" at her acceptance as a pastor. She says the ELCA in general is very concerned about representation of women on committees and other forms of equality.

"About half of seminary graduates are women and close to half of all active clergy in ELCA are women." She cites the most current edition (March 3, 2016) of *The Journal of Lutheran Ethics: Women's Ordination,* which honors forty-five years of ordaining women in the ELCA and its predecessor churches, with articles written by both clergywomen and clergymen. She says, "Things are becoming very equal." However, she says, senior pastors are still usually men, partly because many women seminary graduates are still at a newer stage of their careers. "I think only one ELCA church in Virginia with multiple pastors has a female senior pastor."

St. Luke's in Culpeper is Kate's first pastoral call. She arrived at a time when the church was in transition. There had already been a female pastor there, so Kate's gender was not a surprise to the congregation that ultimately called her. However, being both female and young was a hurdle for some. A few were "shocked by my sheer presence, being both young and female," as one parishioner commented to her. Kate believes that her presence can open doors for people to see the Gospel in a new way. "It can be refreshing to see something different."

After years of running a successful kindergarten through eighth grade school, times had changed and the school at St. Luke's was no longer economically viable. The closing of the school was difficult for the congregation, causing a painful split when the school was sold to the Catholic church in Culpeper. Kate likens it to a divorce in a family, saying she came into the conflict seeing her role to bring stabilization and love to the church community. "I saw no sense in fighting over what had been. I wanted us to center ourselves on the Gospel, on worship and Christian education, not what had been in the past."

She embraces the motto of St. Luke's, "We are a part of the body of Christ, sharing God's love, serving all people." She found herself the clergy-leader of a large building that used to house the school but now had many rooms sitting useless. She now has dual and complementary roles of being first the worship leader, but also the manager of a facility fulfilling many purposes within the community at large. There are fifteen sizable classrooms, a kitchen, a few offices, assorted other rooms, and a large, light-filled sanctuary.

Part of the transformation of the building has been to rename rooms to reflect their current use. For example, the old choir room is now the "Gathering Room" to show its current function as a meeting place. The old school office is now the "Upper Room" and has been rededicated for prayer and reflection. The old music room is now the "Power Pack Room" and houses the makings for 1,200 weekend meals for children on free and reduced lunch status at their schools.

Worshippers coming to service see a large banner Kate has resurrected from the old school days which depicts an ox, the symbol of St. Luke. She sees this original banner of the congregation as important in transitioning from a school into a church, blending the what-was-then with the what-is-now. The sanctuary has long pews on both sides of a center aisle.

Tall windows of clear glass line the exterior walls, and Kate says when she preaches, she often gestures to scenes outside the window—the beauty of nature, the presence of neighbors, other such views. Dressed in her white vestments, adorned with the stole of the season and a brilliant gold cross around her neck, flanked by white-clad acolytes and others involved in the service, Kate conducts exploration of the Gospel as her congregation worships.

St. Luke's is growing and Kate is very conscious of the needs of her various parishioners. She knows that youth are sometimes lost from church participation after they graduate from high school as they become busy young college students, professionals and parents. She is also well aware that the church is graying, so she strives to keep people from all parts of the age spectrum involved in church activities. A church CareGivers group tends those in need, updating the prayer list, sending cards, providing dinners for sick or grieving members, and informing Kate of pastoral care needs. A group called LAFF (Lutheran Adults, Fun & Fellowship) appears, from pictures posted on the website, to be composed primarily of older parishioners.

Kate has successfully advocated to have child care be available so that more young parents can be involved in church activities, not just worship. St. Luke's has youth as full voting members on its governing council, hoping to transmit the idea that church involvement is not limited to youth activities. She also believes young people should be involved as readers and assisting ministers, not just acolytes.

The most satisfying part of her work is "being a part of people's stories, being present, representing the Gospel in word and by presence." She loves being a part of her community of Culpeper. She has prayed at the opening of Town Council and Board of Supervisors' meetings and participated in candle-lighting ceremonies at the hospital. She is active in domestic violence work and belongs to the North Piedmont Virginia Interfaith Center for Public Policy, an advocacy group.

As Kate is part of the community, so is St. Luke's. In an effort to fulfill the Gospel through community use of the abundant space in the building, Kate has assumed a building manager role. She now asks questions such as, "Does our insurance cover that?" and does other things, she says with a laugh, that she was not taught in seminary.

The building is used for a wide range of community activities. It is a homeless shelter established by the local ministerial association—a couple of former classrooms are filled with cots and bedding—and that ministry has recently hired a part-time coordinator for the shelter. Community grants provide dental care and hygiene assistance for the homeless, and Kate has been on the steering committee of that venture. Six Boy and Girl Scout troops, a robotics club, and a yoga group meet at the church. GED (high school diploma equivalency program) classes in Spanish meet in one classroom and Seventh Day Adventists worship in the sanctuary on Saturdays. The church also hosts a community food closet and Agape Counseling and Therapeutic Services. A glance at the crowded monthly church usage calendar details these and other activities.

A few months ago, Kate assumed a new role when her son was born to her and her husband, Jon, whom she met at the College of William and Mary. She says the infant, three and a half months old at the time of the interview, is a "congregation baby," a part of the life of the congregation. "I'm learning to blend parts of my life," she says. "I learn every day now. The congregation is thrilled, threw us a huge shower, gave me two more weeks of maternity leave than required by my contract. I love working, though enjoyed my nine weeks at home. I'm not made to be a stay-at-home mom."

Kate's sister is serving as a live-in nanny at present, though on the day of the interview, the infant was in the church office sleeping in his carriage. He woke happily and sat on his mother's lap for about half the interview, smiling and engaging throughout the time. She describes one Sunday when her husband was ill so she brought the infant with her to church, confident that "if I showed up, someone would watch him." Indeed, she had many offers of child care so the baby was well tended while Kate conducted worship.

"Not everyone wants her baby to be involved in the church. Some pastors want to separate their roles. He provides me a new way to minister in my community. People tell me stories now they wouldn't have before." She is looking forward to her former campus pastor coming soon to baptize her baby.

While Kate has not ever felt a strong separation from God herself, she says, "I expect there will come a time, a dark night." Sometimes she feels that she has shifted from being a worshipper in the pews to "the other side." She says, "I never get to sing the last line of a hymn anymore [because she's getting ready for what happens next]. I sometimes feel I administer worshipping instead of worshipping myself." One of the things she enjoyed about her maternity leave was being able to be a worshipper instead of a leader, "almost a worship sabbatical."

If she had it to do over again, Kate would definitely become a pastor. Her advice to young women contemplating the clergy: "Share the Gospel, preach the Word!"

CHAPTER 14
Donna

DONNA JARVIS, FIFTY-SIX, IS an elder at New Destiny Baptist Church and a chaplain at Medi Home Health and Hospice in Fredericksburg, VA. She is also founder and CEO of the nonprofit charity Outside the Walls Christian Ministry.

"Nursing and ministry marry well in hospice," says the Reverend Doctor Donna Jarvis. Living her earlier years in difficult circumstances, she has dedicated herself to serving others as a nurse, a clergywoman and a counselor.

Born and raised on Long Island, NY, she grew up with two brothers and two sisters and describes her home as "church-going but not Christian." As a child Donna loved going to church, sometimes to the point that she met resistance from her parents. They might plan a family outing for Sunday that Donna refused to attend because she knew she belonged in church every Sunday. She says she knew no female ministers as a child and did not think of this career for herself, especially since she was a shy, quiet child.

Life changed abruptly when both her parents died when she was eighteen, three months apart. Not knowing what else to do, she soon married and found herself pregnant in an abusive marriage. She says, "I was very young, very naïve." She had isolated herself from her family until the day her husband told her, "I will shove a gun up your vagina and kill you."

Fear for her unborn child caused Donna to seek help from her family. "I reconnected with my family when [my husband] told me my day of death and how I would die. By the grace of God I escaped."

Family members put her on a bus to other relatives in Virginia to get her away from the domestic violence, literally saving her life. "I was pregnant and had one pair of shoes and one maternity outfit." Her family took her in and she went to social services for help. "It was the most degrading experience ever. I was sent to a room to rummage through bags for clothes. My self-esteem couldn't have been lower. I wanted to make sure other women would never feel that way." This experience led to the establishment of Donna's outreach charity, Outside the Walls, many years later in 2010, ministering to families in crisis, especially domestic violence.

Working as a nurse's aide and marrying Ray, her current husband of thirty-seven years, led Donna to her degrees and career in nursing. She went to work as a nurse's aide when she had three children not yet of school age—she now has four children and five grandchildren—and discovered she loved geriatrics. She was at first resistant to studying nursing, remembering how much she'd hated chemistry in high school.

After ten years of nurse's aide work, she went to nursing school at the age of thirty. Her career in nursing spanned many years and many jobs, including being nursing administrator at Coffeewoods Correctional Center, a prison for men near Culpeper, VA. Until recently, she was nursing case manager at

Medi Home Health and Hospice in Fredericksburg. In 2015 she became the full-time chaplain with the organization.

Donna has worked in the nursing field for thirty-two years and was called into ministry several years later. She has her bachelor's and master's degrees in nursing from George Mason University in Fairfax, VA; a master's of divinity degree from Baptist Theological Seminary at Richmond; and a doctorate in Christian counseling from Andersonville Baptist Seminary in Camilla, GA. She has melded the disciplines of nursing, ministry and counseling to fashion her career.

Her biggest stumbling block to becoming a minister later turned into her best support—her husband, Ray. She recalls they were going through a "rough season in our marriage" when she began to feel a strong call to become part of a local church. She attended Mt. Olive Baptist Church in Stafford, VA, at that time and says, "I believe God was calling me into ministry to preach but I wasn't ready to accept." She applied to take an on-line course because "I thought maybe that would be enough to show I was not ready for such a high calling by God."

Donna says, "I would cry every day. I could hear God calling but didn't have the support of my husband." She remembers that her husband was jealous: "My time was not his time anymore. I did it all, school, kids, home. I took care of everybody." In 1999 she joined the church and became very active in ministry there.

Driving to the prison where she worked quite a few miles away, she cried every day as she drove. "I woke up crying every night. I heard God talking to me, heard God say 'Genesis 9,' the story of Noah, God's covenant of the rainbow. I still didn't understand."

About that time Donna had to fly to Tennessee for training for her work. She'd never flown alone before and was in a very small airplane. She pulled the window shade down to block out the storm raging outside the plane.

A voice told her, "Put up the shade."

Donna says, "We were above the clouds and I saw double rainbows. I knew God was saying, 'You got to do this and I'll be with you.'"

She explained to her husband what had transpired. "He gave me a look, not saying no but not feeling it." She explains that her husband's father was a Baptist minister and he knew firsthand the hardship imposed on a minister's family.

"The more I tried not to, the more guilt I felt day by day," Donna says. "I finally said yes. My greatest stumbling block in the beginning [my husband] is my greatest supporter now. I had to learn to balance and not neglect anything, had to take on roles of wife, mother, working and school. My bed partner was books, had to push them aside to sleep."

Presently in ministry, Donna serves as an elder at New Destiny Baptist Church in Fredericksburg. Elders are responsible to the pastor for the spiritual nurturing and feeding of the church. This role includes praying, teaching, preaching and counseling. It is an unpaid position at which she serves at least twenty hours a week, including preparation for teaching and preaching. In her role as elder, Donna is the exaltation pastor for New Destiny's contemporary worship service, currently held on Saturday evenings.

Donna describes New Destiny Baptist "as a church plant, a newly established church now in its fifth year. The church's emphasis is now centered on the theme of 'Making Disciples Who Make a Difference.'"

Donna is known as the Reverend Doctor Donna Jarvis at the church. She preaches on a rotation basis with other ministers at

New Destiny. She doesn't wear a robe, though she did when she first began preaching in 2006. If she preaches during the traditional service, she wears a suit—"I'm more confident in a suit." However, she will most likely be wearing jeans preaching during the contemporary worship service.

She likes to move around when she preaches. She says, "Be prepared for your head to move from side to side when I preach. I start in the pulpit and then move out, don't stand in one spot." She also sings as a part of the worship service on occasion—she loves to sing.

"I've always been one to help. I've always been in a helping profession. I feel called to do more in the community." That feeling led her to complete her doctorate in Christian counseling. She is licensed by the National Christian Counselors Association and is a member of the National Christian Counselors Association, the American Association of Christian Counselors, the Sarasota Academy of Christian Counselors, and the Black American Christian Counselors.

Her beliefs and her own past negative experiences led her to establish Outside the Walls, a nonprofit faith-based charity in Stafford. The ministry operates on donations and, according to the brochure, specializes in "rendering services to those in need (women, children, and families) ... by the unified and collaborative efforts of faith-based organizations, community businesses, and Christians showing the love of Christ through education and service."

Counseling is offered, paid for by donations, for "individuals, couples, youth, children, and families ... in the areas of depression, anxiety, fear, marital problems, family conflict, grief, pre-marital counseling, and many others. God has the solution to your problems." Donna's husband, daughter and son-in-law also work with her in Outside the Walls.

Originally Donna's intent was to work primarily with women and children snared in domestic abuse. "I wanted them to feel free of domestic violence, giving them needed counseling, help them be able to forgive. I wanted to give something more, help them to heal." While Outside the Walls has offered a wide array of services in the past, the clothing closet is closing down as they shift their emphasis to children and concentrate more on grief counseling.

Regarding her work, Donna says, "There's a fine line between ministry and counseling. The issues people deal with, patients and families, stress, caregiver role changes between parents and children, families who don't want to let go. My job [at hospice] supports my heart [Outside the Walls]. God planned it that way. It's all connected."

As she began serving in the church, she recognized that "the obstacle that many women faced was acceptance by male clergy. Women were not in the pulpit. During that time, women [doing the] preaching were usually seen on Women's Day once a year."

Donna always had someone to guide her as a mentor—but always male—who "were always showing me how I should be doing something different. Learning and understanding my call by God gave me confidence the Holy Spirit would lead me."

The role of women in ministry is changing, Donna believes. "It's shifting to greater acceptance." Acceptance by others was the great obstacle she faced when she became a member of the clergy. She wanted to please people and to be accepted, needed to know she was important to people.

The closest she ever came to a crisis in her own faith was when her marriage was under strain and she was trying to fix things. A wall built up between her and others and God. "I wasn't going to allow anyone to hurt me. Spiritually I was not trusting

God, making no progress in my life. I asked, 'Why aren't You helping me?' I was crying on the way to work and pulled my car over. God said, 'Trust me.' I was telling people to trust God but not doing it myself. My faith connected to what I could see, then I began to see."

Donna says, "Hurt in your life—those experiences shape us. I became hurt and healed and that allows me to help others. Our experiences are not the end of us but they shape us. Sometimes I have a lack of patience. My kids say, 'I'm asking you to be my mom, not my counselor.'"

Her most rewarding moments are when she sees breakthroughs at work with her hospice patients. She tells of one woman with early-onset dementia who had little contact with the world anymore. "I love to sing. I was playing hymns and put headphones on her. Her face lit up when she heard the music, a nonverbal reaction of joy. When I see God has turned things around, that gives me the most joy."

She sometimes feels frustrated at her lack of time, such as when she prepares her sermons. That takes her away from other things that might be important. "Big things always happen around the time I preach. I miss out on family things because I'm not in control of my time. That was one of the things I had to learn, how to budget and balance the gift of time."

Family time is very important to Donna, especially now that her husband is encountering serious health problems. They observe a traditional Sunday family dinner with their grown children every week. She is "very intentional and purposeful" in keeping family ties very strong in this time of crisis for them. Donna remains close to other family members, too. One of her brothers became a Jehovah's Witness and she laughs and says, "We don't talk religion." A sister once declared herself an atheist, shocking to Donna then, but that sister now attends church. When it was time for Donna to be ordained, she recalls her family's reaction as, "Nobody was against it."

If she could do her career over, she says, "I would have started seminary younger. However, I understand more. I'm still learning daily. A lot of things I experienced in seminary made sense later." She found a strong support group of women in seminary and is still in touch with many of them.

Donna's advice to women headed for the clergy is, "If God is calling you, you can't resist. Be aware and be in balance. Being a minister doesn't erase everything else a woman does. It doesn't take away other roles."

The brochure for Outside the Walls advises, "You don't have to see the whole staircase. Just take the first step." Donna has taken many first steps in her life and continues to help others find their paths.

CHAPTER 15
Mary

MARY HENDERSON, SEVENTY-ONE, IS a retired United Church of Christ minister who maintained her career as a chaplain.

"I like working within an institution, being a part of an overall team. Running the show was never who I am. I like being of service, helping people feel more nearly whole, helping them reconcile."

This sums up how Mary spent her days—and often nights—as a clergywoman working in three continuous-care retirement facilities (independent living, assisted living, nursing, and dementia care on one campus) and in two hospitals with Level 1 (the highest designation for a hospital) trauma units. Rather than become pastor of a congregation, Mary opted to become a clinical chaplain through taking clinical pastoral education training, certified by the Association of Professional Chaplains.

She laughs and says, "I'm a champion hoop-jumper," referring to her success in working within the church, various certification agencies and health care organizations.

Mary grew up in a family that attended church, though she says they were "pretty casual churchgoers. In the 1950s you needed to do that [go to church]." They usually attended Methodist churches and sometimes base chapels as they moved around for her father's military career. Mary's father was a Navy pilot and her mother, a Navy nurse, both deployed to combat areas after Pearl Harbor.

The church formed a moral and ethical compass for Mary in her early years. A spiritual journey group when she was a teenager helped define her spirituality. She taught Sunday school and was active in a spiritual group on Staten Island. She matriculated at Hunter College, which was an all-women's college until her senior year when men were admitted, majoring in French, minoring in education and art history. Somewhere during her college years, "I decided God was dead," Mary says with a laugh.

She earned a graduate degree in library science at SUNY-Albany and began working in museums, first the Munson-Williams-Proctor Art Institute in Utica, NY, and then the John G. White Collection in Cleveland, known for its early books in the areas of chess and checkers and a huge international collection of folklore. While she enjoyed the museum jobs, she found the specialized collections work did not provide as much contact with people as she wished.

She moved to the Cleveland Heights branch of the public library and became a community librarian, the public face of the local branch. She visited nursing homes, city hall and other places to represent the library. She discovered she enjoyed working with a wide variety of people.

After moving with her son and first husband to Washington, DC, she worked in retail for a brief time and suddenly found herself a single mother with a young son after her marriage dissolved. She worked herself back into a library science job with a private company that specialized in technology to link government agencies and other entities.

During the time she was single, "I was busy being an atheist," she says. She was struggling to live on her own with her young son and found herself depressed as her life turned out not at all as she had expected. In time she began dating and was surprised to find herself dating some single ministers she met at Parents Without Partners. She used to say to them, "This is so strange. You serve God, but I don't believe at all." This naturally led to discussions about faith and they gave her books to read on religion, including several written by contemporary theologians.

"One day I was sitting on my porch and I heard church bells ringing from the nearby Methodist church where my son attended day care. I had a life-changing experience of God's presence and a sense of call to return to church and to enter the ministry. I thought I was really going crazy but I could not deny the power of that experience over me. It was transforming."

She went inside and asked her young son, "Alex, would you like to go to church with me?" and received the answer, "'Mommy, I've been waiting for you to ask me.' What an affirmation!"

Mary knew the associate pastor, only a few years younger than herself, from her connection with the church's day care program. "I sobbed my way through the first service. They were lovely to me. I was afraid I had gone totally nuts, acting on the voice I had heard. My realities were bumping up against each other."

She became an active member right away, joining prayer and study groups and says of the time, "They embraced me like family. They sensed the depth and sincerity of my faith and enthusiasm, but I never told anyone about my ministerial call. I scrambled to catch up. I didn't know my Bible. My son had kids to play with at the church and it was a wonderful, affirming experience for me. After awhile they asked me to take over Christian education and I was proud and happy to do so."

Mary says of the turmoil in her life then, "I got down to my core values. I had married for life, sacrificed for his education and career [when he asked for divorce]. I was completely unprepared to be a single parent and had to struggle on my own without much emotional support outside my new church family. I didn't have a goal. My self-concept was low. Counseling helped me find myself.

"A few years later I met Ron, who had been raised in the very fundamental Church of Christ which he had left as a teenager." Ron had had no contact with the church in the interim but he was interested in faith and a church that was closer to his own more progressive theology.

They married and the family moved to Silver Spring, MD. They searched for but did not find a Methodist church they wanted to attend but instead discovered a United Church of Christ (UCC) congregation two blocks away. "There we both felt we were at home."

It was a large church with many program opportunities. They joined the marriage enrichment retreats and support groups for men and women and blended families. Mary taught junior high Sunday school classes and over time both took church leadership positions. The church's youth orchestra appealed to her trumpet-playing son, as did summer church camp in the West Virginia hills. They found a lot of ways to fit in, and the liberal progressive values and social justice programs of that congregation felt just right for them.

The clergywoman who was associate pastor at that church

became one of Mary's role models. After a class in meditation, Mary enrolled in the Shalem Institute and took classes. She worked with a spiritual director and confided that she had a call. Her spiritual director asked her, "And what are you going to do about it?"

Mary says, "That she would take me seriously rocked my world."

Then in her forties, Mary knew she was called to enter service of some kind, perhaps social work, health administration or chaplaincy. She had quit her full-time job in the library world. Instead she volunteered at a hospice and began working part-time at an AZT hotline. (AZT, azidothymidine, is an antiretroviral drug used to treat and prevent HIV/AIDS.) Her stepson had contracted AIDS so Mary was deeply invested in the work.

In time she switched to the Cancer Information Service Hotline and eventually became librarian to the project. During this time of discernment, she did some more therapy and also meditated, prayed and kept a journal, trying to figure out what she was going to do with her life. After much soul-searching, she decided she felt most strongly called to the chaplaincy.

The stumbling block was she had to become a minister to do so. She never believed she was called to lead a congregation but rather "to work with people in pain, to listen, encourage, to be there." Accepting the role as spiritual leader was hard for her. Eventually she resolved in her mind and heart to become a chaplain with all that entailed. Her pastor urged her to go to seminary.

Wesley Theological Seminary accepted her mid-year. The admissions process was a disappointment to her. "After I had spent a multitude of hours prayerfully and thoughtfully preparing my application, I heard simply, 'Yes, you can start.'" This felt to her like a shallow response to her own deep spiritual investment.

Most of what she heard at the seminary was lectures on all-inclusive language, the hot topic of that time, with little mention of other issues facing Christianity. However, she found inspiration from Rabbi Ed Friedman's class on applying Bowen family systems theory to congregations. Her husband, Ron, audited the class as well. They both liked the professor and decided to do couples' therapy with "Uncle Eddie."

"I still struggled to accept my call as a spiritual leader," Mary says, "and I was eager to test it out in a health care-based ministry." That summer she began her first unit of clinical pastoral education, the most recognized form of training for chaplains in the health professions. She entered the program at St. Elizabeth's Hospital, an institution for the mentally ill in Washington, DC.

There she met a lot of people from Howard University School of Divinity, a historically black university in the nation's capital, a nondenominational, very diverse Protestant seminary. She thought she might like to transfer there. In her admission interview, Dean Laurence Jones spent a couple of hours with her in a spiritual discernment process. He said at the conclusion, "Well, Mrs. Henderson, if you believe God is calling you to Howard Seminary, you're in!"

Mary says, "It felt a lot more personal and spiritual than the Wesley equivalent."

She liked the idea of training with people from various cultures, which she saw as good preparation for the populations she'd find in health care settings. She knew she'd be in a minority herself and found that instructive as well. Only four percent of the students were obviously Caucasian but about half were women. She found a warm welcome there, she recalls.

"At Howard, I'd get hugged from the front door to the classroom every time I arrived." A few people did wonder out loud why she was taking up a spot a black student "could/should have had," but overall she says she was made to feel very welcome by students and faculty.

She received a Ford Fellowship, a free ride for a year, participated in multi-racial worship, and learned black church history. "I sat awed in homiletics classes with fellow students who had preached for years who were back for their academic degrees."

She was chosen to participate in a United Nations program in New York City. She says, "I had not expected all those extras. I was surprised to find my fellow seminarians saw me as part of a 'persecuted gender.' I had always considered myself a privileged woman to have lived in the feminist era, but at Howard I began to look at myself in that way for the first time. In my courses, I was learning more about how the 'isms'—racism, classism, elitism."

Mary recalls, "While I did expect to be a minority race-wise, I realized I was part of a persecuted minority [women] and began to look at myself in that way. I had never been a bra-burner. I knew I wanted to be a chaplain and planned my courses that way."

She received her master's of divinity degree from Howard and was planning a career as a hospital chaplain. To move towards that goal, she had accepted a residency year in a hospital that lost funding for their clinical pastoral education (CPE) program at the last minute. Suddenly, she had no place to go and all the other options were filled up.

She spent another month searching her soul about her calling and then, she says, "Miraculously, a new position for a CPE residency at the Asbury Methodist Village in Gaithersburg, MD, opened up. I discovered I felt a great deal of affinity for older people and did well with people both in independent living and dementia care."

She planned worship but didn't have to preach all the time: "It takes me a long time to prepare a sermon and makes me anxious to preach," she confesses. "I much prefer the counseling, praying, consoling part of the work."

She was ordained by the United Church of Christ when she received her first call after her year-long residency in 1992. The Altenheim Community in Indianapolis, from the Evangelical and Reformed Tradition of the UCC, offered Mary a job as a chaplain, so she and her husband moved to Indiana. By then her son was in college. She enjoyed her time there where she preached about once a month and more often served as the liturgist, inviting the pastors of the residents to participate in the worship. This kept the services ecumenical and the residents were thrilled to show off their own pastors to their friends.

Mary also enjoyed designing special services for anniversaries, dedications, Christmas pageants and vow renewals, as well as healing services, bedside communions, Seder meals and other such services. She loved to teach Bible study. She mostly did pastoral care, focusing on the "three D issues: dying, depression, and dementia," working as well with family and some staff issues.

Mary especially valued the times she helped patients near the end of their lives reconcile conflict with others. She remembers one woman who had been sexually abused by her father, who vigorously denied it. "They had not spoken for years," says Mary, "and the daughter felt she had only this last chance to hear him say he was sorry."

Mary worked with both of them and finally the father said, "I never meant to hurt her," which sent the woman weeping into Mary's office with a sense of vindication and healing. "The father felt relieved by his confession and joy at the reconciliation. He died in peace," Mary says.

Another time a woman with dementia asked for confession and absolution. In a moment of apparent lucidity, she confided to Mary that her son was not the son of her husband, and she wanted God to forgive her and to tell her son the truth. Days later, the son came to Mary's office and told her, "I'm glad to know. I always suspected that." Mary says, "You never know when reconciling moments will happen."

She worked there for eight years and enjoyed good relationships with the other pastors with whom she served. However, she felt lonely being six hundred miles away from her family and unable to travel to them very often because of the demands of her job. "I felt I had met all the challenges I could meet in that situation so I started looking for another job," she says.

She became senior staff chaplain in the Phoebe Home in Allentown, PA, a population of almost eight hundred souls in various stages of elderly life. Mary says, "It was way too huge. In addition to all those pastoral needs, I was site supervisor of all clinical chaplain trainees. We eventually hired another person to help, but I felt like a stranger in the Pennsylvania Dutch culture. I didn't know the culture, didn't speak German, and worked ten to twelve hours a day. I never felt welcome, didn't feel satisfaction."

Her supervisor once told her, "You don't make me feel relaxed." Mary told her husband, "I can't stand this," to which he replied, "Find something else."

Her next position was a year-long chaplain residency program at St. Luke's Hospital in Bethlehem, PA. "I really enjoyed it. I love trauma center work, the adrenaline thing. I thought, 'Maybe I'll work in a hospital yet.'"

Then her husband persuaded her that they should buy an RV, travel for awhile to celebrate his new retirement freedom, and then she should look for a new job. After some time traveling, she had several interviews and settled on a job at Lake Prince Woods Retirement Community in Suffolk, VA, a not-for-profit organization of the United Church Homes and Services, affiliated with the United Church of Christ. She became director of spiritual life and loved her job.

She says, "I 'get' Southern culture in all its peculiarities. It's so different from the Pennsylvania Dutch community. It was a great ministry for me for seven years."

She had promised her husband she'd retire when she turned sixty-five. They enjoyed a big RV trip to celebrate her retirement and then moved to a Del Webb over-fifty-five community in Fredericksburg, VA. They enjoy living near family, which includes several grandchildren and great-grandchildren, and being in a place with a sense of community.

Mary is a master gardener and manages a butterfly garden for her area. She enjoys quilting and playing bridge. She attends the local UCC church and is in discussion with other retired ministers where she lives about beginning an ecumenical service one Sunday a month in their community. She has agreed to preach one Sunday in four.

She has some advice for those contemplating becoming clergywomen. "Seek supporters and mentors in whatever ministry you're called to. They can help you network, tell you the inside story, act as a sounding board, help you find employment opportunities. You have to be a strong person, have a strong call. Ignore people such as one guy who said to me, 'You can't be a chaplain, you're a woman.'"

She advises, "Get the formal education, the certifications, the ordination. These will open doors for you. And, if you can, be prepared to go where the job is."

When she retired from the chaplaincy, her supervisor

reminded her she'd previously been given three symbols of clinical pastoral care: a tambourine (referencing Miriam, for leading the people), some purple cloth (Lydia, showing devotion to the church), and a jar of ointment (Mary, for healing and comforting). When she ceremonially returned them at her retirement, she said, "No other position in ministry has given me greater joy."

CHAPTER 16
Betsy

BETSY HAAS, FIFTY-SIX, ENTERED seminary at the age of twenty-nine and is ordained as a minister in the United Methodist Church (UMC).

Betsy blazes trails.

She has had the courage to follow her own heart most of her life. Now her life is dedicated to helping others find their own paths to God.

Preaching in the summer heat to a congregation comprising faithful regulars and summer visitors at the beach, the Rev. Betsy Haas, associate pastor of Kitty Hawk (NC) United Methodist Church, poses a striking figure. She wears a semi-fitted long white alb with panels embroidered in crosses. A small UMC symbol of a cross with rising tongues of flame hangs around her neck. Her fashionably styled short hair and skillful use of cosmetics present a professional demeanor. Presiding over worship, she is serious but chatty, warm and high energy as she leads the congregation through the opening exercises.

The church sanctuary is light and airy with large stained-glass windows fashioned of rough-cut chunks of colored glass depicting religious scenes. Red carpet and well-cushioned light-colored wood pews make a bright and welcoming atmosphere. Racks under the pews hold three hymnals, one of which is large-print. A small summer-size choir occupies one corner near the organ, and the senior and associate pastors in their summer-white vestments sit at the front of the church.

To begin the service, some in the congregation rise when invited to report joys of their week: a couple departing for two weeks of African ministry, improved health news for others, for which the congregants applaud. Betsy asks that prayer requests be written on a slip of paper and passed to the ushers.

She delivers her sermon from the floor of the sanctuary rather than from the pulpit, standing just a few feet from the front pews. She speaks without notes and maintains firm eye contact with her listeners—no hiding from this pastor. Her message is based on the text from Samuel in the Old Testament when a young David is unexpectedly selected to be king of Israel after more apparently worthy candidates have been rejected. This text exemplifies her own view of service to God: He picks you and you'd best answer properly, regardless of your preparation and view of your own worthiness.

She begins with a story that captures the congregation's attention, moves through explanation of the Biblical text, salts her talk with observations from Malcolm Gladwell's *Blink*, and covers her points quickly and thoroughly. In just a few minutes she explicates her text, introduces her theme, throws in some mildly feminist and non-homophobic comments, adjures us all to be nonjudgmental of viewpoints with which we disagree, and urges soccer moms to bring their kids to church instead of soccer tournaments on Sundays. It is a moving and effective message of faith and call to service.

At one point she asks, "Can I get a witness?" to which the

congregation choruses "Amen." When asked about that later, Betsy laughs and says, "I taught them that." She explains that her adult years in the South exposed her to diverse congregations and she adopted that phrase for her repertoire. She closes the service with a modern hymn written by a woman.

Betsy's faith journey began when she was a child in the Methodist church where she grew up in New Jersey. When she was eleven, she attended a lay witness retreat. This ministry is a fifty-five-year-old tradition in the United Methodist Church, according to an article in the July 23, 2010, edition of *Good News Magazine*, a publication "Leading United Methodists to a Faithful Future." Betsy was unknowingly a trailblazer in a relatively young movement within her church, founded with the idea that laypersons speak to laypersons through testimony, based on the tradition of church revivals.

At that weekend event in her childhood, she had an "altar call moment, my own conversion" and "walked the aisle" to declare her faith. Her experience was so significant that she went into training to become a lay witness, blazing more trails at the young age of twelve. She began speaking publicly of her faith at lay witness retreats and credits this experience with giving her confidence in speaking in public, as well as stating her faith.

She recalls that she "didn't mind standing before the group when I was twelve to explain my own conversion experience." She laughs that she was astounded and said to a friend many years later, "Shut the front door! You mean everyone doesn't want to speak in public?" upon learning that most of the world doesn't enjoy speaking in front of a group. Her mother, a financial officer of a school system, spoke often in public as did her father, who performed in barbershop quartets, and she believes their stage presence was a model for her own comfort.

About the time Betsy was "coming into her own personal relationship with God," her parents had a falling-out over the congregational issue of whether or not the pastor should be removed from the church the family attended. They thought he was being treated unfairly and felt very bitter and disillusioned. They left the church and never returned. Betsy, however, continued in attendance, walking to services every Sunday by herself. It was a somewhat confusing time for her as she was gaining her faith at the same time it appeared to her that her parents were losing theirs. She continued to attend services through her middle school and early high school years.

In high school Betsy was a member of the marching band. She played clarinet and bassoon and took up tenor sax to join the "jazz band with the cute boys." Her junior year of high school, she blazed a new trail as the first female drum major for her band. She believes the excellent coaching she received for that role and the opportunity for leadership were influential in her later life. The band performed in competitions all over the Jersey shore so she began missing church on Sundays and fell away a bit from her previous religious life.

Betsy matriculated at Penn State University to study journalism. At her freshman orientation, she was introduced to a sophomore named Kenn Haas, and they have been together ever since. She and Kenn, the son of a Navy family, later flew to London to meet his family where they were stationed. She remembers her parents footing the bill for a plane ticket because they were "big on education and travel." She loved the time in London and got her first view of the life she would lead for several years as the wife of a Naval officer.

Because Kenn was a year ahead of her, Betsy blazed through Penn State in three years, a very stressful endeavor, she recalls.

She received her degree at the same time he did and became a Navy wife as Kenn began fulfilling his seven-year Navy obligation after being an ROTC student. She loved their Navy years, from his pilot training at Pensacola to billets in California and Texas. She relates, "I adjusted to moves and separations, I loved Navy life."

Throughout those years Betsy was involved in church wherever they lived. Kenn's family was also Methodist and the couple had continued their church attendance while they were in college. Sometimes during their Navy stint they attended Methodist churches; sometimes, base chapels.

Betsy directed the choir in one base chapel, drawing on her childhood voice lessons and her high school drum major experience. She had to learn not to wave her arms as dramatically in a small chapel as a drum major does on a large field, but she says the principle is the same. She enjoyed that time because the Disciples of Christ Navy chaplain and she were theologically congruent. She played in a hand bell choir in a Texas church and substituted for the choir director there.

Betsy held several jobs based on her education at Penn State. Her favorite was director of student life in a community college in Texas. She managed a dorm and "chased drunk cowboys off the campus at three in the morning." She had worked as a resident advisor while a student at Penn State so was familiar with the work this job required. She later did public relations for a credit union and display advertising for a newspaper in California. Though she was never a reporter, she used her journalism background in these jobs.

Betsy was surprised when Kenn received an offer from Delta Airlines and they decided to leave the Navy; she had thought their Navy life would be a career. The couple moved to the

Atlanta area for his new job as a Delta pilot and immediately became involved in Peachtree City United Methodist Church. She recalls this as "a wonderful time in my life." She held various jobs in this church, both paid and unpaid, including director of Christian education and eventually was the senior member of the associate pastors after she finished seminary and was ordained.

With two young daughters, Betsy became a stay-at-home mom, and at the Peachtree City church she became part of a tight-knit group of young mothers. A shy friend, scared to go alone, asked her to attend Disciple Bible Study, "a program of disciplined Bible study aimed at developing strong Christian leaders." (www.cokesbury.com)

Her friend said, "I can be quiet and you speak and besides, they have a free nursery." Betsy laughs and says, "If they hadn't had a free nursery, I wouldn't be a pastor today."

She recalls that somewhere around the seventeenth lesson in the Disciple study, they read the line, "'God seeks the least, the last, and the lost,' and it hit me like a thunderbolt and I thought, 'That's exactly me!'" She heard, as when calling the original Disciples, "God doesn't call the equipped, he equips the called." She said, "I knew my whole life had brought me to that moment, knew all was coming into one place."

At the conclusion of the study, her pastor asked her to teach the next course so she went to a hotel in Atlanta to get training. She sat next to a seminary student who was studying at Emory University and a whole new possibility opened up for her. Having lived in Atlanta only a short time, she didn't know there was a nearby seminary.

About the same time, her pastor unexpectedly called on her to do a children's sermon. Whoever was supposed to do it hadn't shown up. Betsy recalls she was sitting "minding my own business in my choir robe, counting the ceiling tiles" when he turned to her and said, "Okay, Betsy, give us a children's sermon."

The choir had earlier been practicing the seven-fold amen and she'd been thinking how much prettier the soprano part was than the humdrum bass role. So she got up in front of the assembled children, turned to the choir, and asked them to help her: "I knew they'd help." She had the basses do their part individually, then the baritones, tenors, altos, and sopranos each sang their roles. Then she had them all sing together to produce an amazing blend and told the children, "This is the way God puts us together. The church is better when we all work together," relating it to Paul's idea in the Bible of wholeness.

"The Holy Spirit came on me to give the children's sermon," she says. "God gave me that whole thing. I also trusted the choir. The experience brought a lot of clarity to my call." Afterwards the minister came to her and said, "If you don't go to seminary, you're being disobedient in the highest order."

So three things came together for her: hearing the call in the Disciple Bible Study group, hearing about Emory from the seminarian, and successfully preaching to the children. She also saw the path that had brought her to this moment: She had "walked the aisle" while a lay witness; had led as a drum major; and had moved about and adjusted to new situations as a Navy wife. Everything seemed to coalesce in her mind to point her toward seminary and ordination. She had been told as a child lay witness that she was destined for the ministry but had discounted that, never having seen a female pastor, though the UMC did ordain women at that time.

"I was terrified to tell my husband," Betsy says. "He hadn't known me when I was a lay witness, a young Holy Roller for Jesus, hadn't known me that way. I thought, 'This is going to change my marriage forever.'" She talked to his mother before she talked to him and found great encouragement there. "I finally got up the nerve, said I might have a calling. I'll take some classes, think I might want to be a pastor."

She recalls his words, "I gotta be honest, I never thought about sleeping with a minister." Then he got out the checkbook and wrote a check for seminary.

While Betsy attended Candler School of Theology at Emory University, her church young-mother friends banded together to help with child care for her two preschoolers, then two and four. Her busy husband was not only flying for Delta but also still in the Naval Reserve. Her friends organized pick-ups and after-school care, fed the girls lunch, and provided support crucial to Betsy's achieving her goal. She recalls there was no prouder group at her ordination than the young mothers who'd provided child care so she could earn her degree.

Becoming an ordained minister in the UMC was a grueling process, several years of seminary followed by a three-year-long candidacy. Meetings with committees during candidacy often involved presenting long papers—"a plethora of paperwork," Betsy recalls—on assigned topics, videotaping sermons, and similar tasks.

Betsy had yet another opportunity to blaze a trail. During her years at seminary, the UMC began recognizing two kinds of pastors: elders and deacons. Elders are most often local pastors and itinerant; that is, they change churches when their bishop reassigns them. Deacons often choose a specialty in ministry and secure their own positions, though both are appointed to a church by the bishop. Betsy decided the deaconate was the position for her, since she had a family to consider.

She describes it in a medical analogy: "The elder is like a general practitioner, handling all aspects of a local church. The deacon is like a brain surgeon, doing specialty work, such as Christian education." She knew the choice to be ordained a deacon was also likely a choice to remain an associate pastor. The trade-off for not being itinerant was that she had to find her own jobs. At the time, she said, it was an uphill battle to become a deacon, an emerging professional group, but she achieved that distinction, among the first cohort to do so.

After ordination, Betsy became an associate pastor at Peachtree City UMC. She loved her job, the most senior of three associates working with the senior pastor. Then that minister left, and a new younger male minister came in and dissolved the whole staff, partly for budgetary reasons. Betsy recalls being devastated—"It was killing me on the inside"—even though publicly she supported the pastor's right to make the changes. The other associates, being elders, were given new positions by the bishop. Betsy-the-Deacon had to find her own and ended up on leave for two years.

The family had vacationed for years at Kenn's parents' place at Outer Banks, NC, and Betsy and her husband had just bought their own house, planning to rent it out for about ten years, then retire to the seaside area. In what she describes as a "crazy time," she left the church she loved where her children had grown up, a vibrant church where she supervised a staff of eight people, and coped with losing her job.

Her husband said, "That's it, we're leaving," and they moved to North Carolina. Betsy calls this "prevenient grace—God actively working to woo you to Him before you know what's happening." Kenn currently does his work by hopping a plane in Norfolk two hours north, flying to Detroit, and taking command of his plane and route, often international, from that city.

There were no jobs available for her in the area, so Betsy

began teaching disciple Bible study as a volunteer in the church where she has now served as part-time associate pastor for five years. Being part-time has denied her benefits, housing, and some of the salary her male predecessor made, but it also gives her some flexibility of time.

However, some factors have coalesced recently in her life to enable her to request assignment as associate pastor in the same church, but on an entirely volunteer basis. She has requested permission to return her salary to the church but gain a much more flexible schedule, pioneering a different approach to ministry. Particularly she wants time to spend with her husband, her daughters, and her aging father-in-law, who lives five hours away.

All her adult life Betsy has felt the tug between the demands of family life and her career. She recalls missing trips with her husband and children when they were younger because her pastoral duties at Peachtree UMC kept her at home. She looks now at photos of those trips with herself notably absent and thinks, "Why did I do it that way?"

She recounts a time shortly before her mother's recent death when she realized she was visiting a parishioner in a nursing home who had plenty of other visitors, but had not seen her own mother—, then a resident of an assisted living facility only five minutes from Betsy's house—in a week, though they'd talked often by phone. She turned her car around and went to see her mother rather than the parishioner that day. She points out a beautiful stained glass piece hanging in her office window, a blue-and-white depiction of a bowl of water draped by a towel. As an ordination gift to Betsy, her mother commissioned that piece symbolizing the role of the deacon. She very much feels the presence of her mother and her mother-in-law in her current everyday life and ministry, though both are deceased.

"Ministry is all about unfinished business," she says. "You never get it all done. There are never enough hours, not enough awareness, not enough time to meet congregational expectations. Every night, I feel the tension of eight things left undone." Her advice to women contemplating ministry is, "Don't stop, don't give up, don't let any obstacle get in your way."

Mourning Break: Words of Hope for Those in Grief by Rev. Betsy Haas and Lisa Mahaffey blazes yet another trail for those in grief, which, sooner or later, is virtually everyone. Through personal stories and Biblical references, the book appeals to people trying to find their way through grief.

During the interview for this narrative, Betsy's phone rang several times and she apologized for checking it. Finally the number she was anticipating appeared. She switched on the phone and asked excitedly, "Are you in labor?" Her daughter resignedly replied that she thought she'd never get to that. Betsy eagerly awaits the birth of her first grandchild, a grandson, and expects to hop a Delta plane any day now to her daughter, married to a Navy pilot stationed in San Diego.

Asked if she'll baptize the baby, she says no, explaining that at their wedding, "I was just Mom." She says at this event, she'll just be Nana—no doubt a trail-blazing Nana.

CHAPTER 17
Sister Miriam Elizabeth

SISTER MIRIAM ELIZABETH CUSACK is a member of the Oblate Sisters of St. Francis de Sales (OSFS) and a teacher at Holy Cross Academy in Fredericksburg, VA.

"Take delight in the present moment and always find your happiness where God places you and in doing what the moment requires of you," is a quotation from St. Leonie Aviat, the foundress of the OSFS order. Sister Miriam Elizabeth exemplifies that quote.

She is a small woman clad in a charcoal gray habit and apron with a long black veil hanging down her back, covering most of her hair. A Roman collar and the trim around the veil edge her habit in white. The mid-calf-length habit tops black walking shoes. A large silver cross, the cross she received when she became a full member of the Order, hangs from a black braided cord around her neck. Sister Miriam Elizabeth speaks with an Irish lilt and has a ready smile. She looks a decade or two younger than the age she confidentially reveals, well past the traditional retirement age.

"I walk a lot," she explains, and she moves with graceful energy.

Sister Miriam Elizabeth is from Dublin, Ireland, where she was reared in a Roman Catholic family with thirteen other siblings, nine of them brothers. She was the eleventh child and some of her older siblings had already left home by the time she was a young child. Her family was religious and she attributes to them her early spiritual formation. Her father attended mass every Sunday and her mother, every day. Her father died while she was in high school but her mother lived to see her make her entrance into the OSFS.

Two of her sisters became Dominican nuns and one brother, a Jesuit priest. An aunt was a nun in the Order of the Poor Clares. Sister Miriam Elizabeth does not believe that influenced her choice of vocation, however.

When she was between the ages of twelve and sixteen, she went each summer with a few classmates to Connemara in the western part of Ireland and stayed two or three weeks. All examinations to the university were administered in the Irish language so she and her classmates practiced to become more fluent before they took their exams. Her schooling was conducted by Dominican nuns until she matriculated at Dublin University.

Dublin University prepared Sister Miriam Elizabeth for teaching. She taught for one year at the university after graduation but decided to move on, "not to be stuck with my school." She told her mother she was going to England to teach, much to her mother's dismay. "People at that time thought if you go to England, you lose your faith, it's the end," she says with a laugh.

During her five enjoyable years of teaching in a private school in England, she began to sense that she had a calling to the church. "The only sisters I knew previously were Dominican. At that time they were enclosed and never went out." She did not see herself fitting into that order.

The school where she taught in England had both local day students and boarding students from several European countries. Often the boarding students' parents worked in countries that might not have had the best schools for their children, so they sent their children to England to be educated. The sisters of the OSFS cared for the boarding students. This was Sister Miriam Elizabeth's first contact with the order.

She often questioned the sisters about their lives and learned that their motherhouse was in France where their order had originated. The sisters talked among themselves in French and the young teacher never let them know she, too, spoke French. She just listened and observed them. She found them to be very spiritual, straightforward in manner, and kind. She began to envision herself among their numbers.

The order of the Oblate Sisters of St. Francis de Sales was founded by Father Louis Brisson and Mother Frances de Sales Aviat (www.oblatesisters.org); Mother Leonie Aviat was canonized to sainthood in 2001. The order was founded in Troyes in France in the late 1800s to rescue children from work in the factories and textile mills. The charism of the order still today is teaching and social work. The Oblate sisters went to work in Africa, South America and North America in the late 1800s. The order now supports two schools in America and is affiliated with DeSales University.

When she was about thirty years old, Sister Miriam Elizabeth broke the news to her mother that she thought she had a calling to be a sister, though she herself had been considering it for some years by then. She says, "I waited until I was sure, that I understood everything" before breaking the news to her mother, who still hoped her daughter would return to Ireland. Instead, she was headed to France.

She went to Troyes, to the motherhouse of the order. "There were lots of novices then, about twenty-five women." She became a postulant, entering a period when she participated in the disciplines and rituals of the community but still wore her own clothes and continued to discern her own calling. About a year later she became a novice for a formation year to learn the practice of the vows of poverty, chastity, and obedience.

"After a year I got these clothes," she says, gesturing to her habit, "but I wore a white veil. I professed for one year—my first profession. I could still back out. I then made my final profession after five years and received my cross and black veil." The entire process of entry into the order took about seven years.

Sister Miriam Elizabeth received her first name—Miriam—from her parents at her christening. Her second name, Elizabeth, was conferred on her at her clothing as a novice. That also happened to be her mother's name, which made her mother very happy.

After she became a full-fledged sister of OSFS, the order sent her back to England to teach in the school where she'd formerly served. She knew the preschool through high school institution well and was happy to be assigned to the high school there to teach English and history. Each year she took students to a different foreign country to visit for a couple of weeks, including some trips to New York City and Washington. She later became principal of this high school.

Some years later, her order assigned her to go to America "since I always said I loved America and I was the only one who spoke English." The British school had fallen on hard economic times due to the mad cow disease and other economic crises, and many parents were unable to pay tuition for their children. School enrollment dropped and it was no longer economically feasible to keep it open. Fewer students meant fewer options in courses so the mother general closed the school and reassigned the sisters.

Sister Miriam Elizabeth was sent to St. Bernadette's School, near Philadelphia. They asked her if she could be the librarian and she said, "Sure, I love books." She became a librarian, taught religion to seventh- and eighth-graders, and started a Spanish program for students in grades six through eight. She went to the American regional house in Childs, MD, to stay in the community from time to time to keep in touch with others of her order.

Her first involvement with the Holy Cross Academy where she now works was as a member of an accreditation team in 2003, when the school was seeking its first accreditation. She returned to Holy Cross in 2010 to teach Spanish and to work in the after-school program, called Aviat Care after the founder of the order. She now lives in a small house adjacent to St. Mary Catholic Church in downtown historic Fredericksburg, VA, with two other sisters of her order. One is a principal and the other, a sixth-grade teacher; all serve Holy Cross Academy.

Sister Miriam Elizabeth could not identify the best part of her work because "I love it all. No matter where I go, I'm happy." She had enjoyed working in a high school, then enjoyed the middle-level grades, but notes that "I never taught little ones." She says the most difficult part of life in a religious order was "leaving behind my family in Ireland when I first entered the order." She spoke about the conflict she felt going away to teach when her mother had wanted her to remain near home.

If she had it to do over again, she'd follow the same path. She believes the years she spent deciding to become a sister were an important time as she thought through the whole obligation. Were she to do it again, she'd still take that time to know her own mind. "If I went in too early, it could have been a problem. I can't imagine going in younger because I loved life—swimming, playing games, tennis. I loved life and my family."

Asked if she'd have become a priest if that path had been open, she replies, "Hard to know" and reiterates that she made a very good choice to be a sister of her order.

Sister Miriam Elizabeth would give this advice to someone considering becoming a sister. "Why do you want this? Have you prayed and do you really have a calling? Are you willing to accept discipline? Especially if you are older, you will know. If it doesn't work, don't stay."

She has experienced some spiritual bleakness in her life. "Everyone goes through darkness. You question, 'Is God real?' In order for your faith to grow, you have to doubt. You investigate, grow and learn." True to her order's creed, she sees adversity as an opportunity for growth.

When asked if she will retire, she explains, "We don't really call it retiring. I'm very happy with what I'm doing but if something happens, that will be okay, too." She acknowledges that she is beyond normal retirement age. "If I felt I couldn't do it, I'd tell them."

She adds with a laugh, "I can't believe my age! How did I get there?" Her activities continue unabated, however. She traveled in 2015 with other "Sisters on Safari," as a newsletter described them, to celebrate the opening of a convent for her order in South Africa.

She concludes philosophically, "Make the best of every day. When I can't, I hope I can accept it."

CHAPTER 18
Christine

CHRISTINE BLICE-BAUM, SIXTY, IS an ordained Lutheran minister. She entered the United States Air Force at the age of forty-one to become a military chaplain.

Call her reverend, lieutenant colonel, doctor or chaplain—she has earned all those titles. Christine is an example of where faith, discipline and curiosity can take one in life. She has already followed at least three career paths as pastor, professor and now Air Force chaplain. She is currently a wing chaplain, a position consistent with her military rank of lieutenant colonel.

A trim, petite stylish woman, Christine carries her air of authority with ease and friendliness. She wears brightly printed leggings of green and turquoise and a black fleece top, complemented with black boots and a turquoise-and-green scarf arranged casually around her neck. Her open smile and well-styled short hair complete a picture of confidence and approachability. She wears her sixty years unbelievably well.

She begins, "I've got two lives, pre-military and military." The first life led naturally into the second, and she is already planning for her next, post-military life. "My journey began in Youngstown, OH, in Steeltown USA," she says. "My parents were not college-educated but they believed in education for me and my older sister." Their belief surely took root in Christine. She holds a bachelor's degree in music, four master's degrees (music, theological studies, divinity, and military art and science) and a doctorate in musical arts.

Music was and remains important in Christine's life. She began taking piano lessons when she was six and playing the organ in churches when she was fifteen. She also played the flute in school. Her music degrees, both the bachelor's and master's in music performance, are from Youngstown State University.

She is a "cradle Lutheran" and her parents were active volunteers in church. Among her earliest memories, she recalls Sundays in the large neo-Gothic-structure church of her childhood. A religious theme, a common thread in her life, began to emerge when she was just a child. She remembers looking out her bedroom window and seeing her mother in conversation with two Roman Catholic sisters, for what reason she can't imagine now. Christine was intrigued with the women dressed in religious garb. That was the beginning of a feeling "almost of yearning" for some sort of religious life. Later she visited a mother-house for sisters of the Lutheran church and thought about "taking this step of faith."

When she began playing the organ in churches, she heard a lot about religion that left her with questions. Her curiosity about the Bible led her eventually to seminary in her early twenties. At that time, she had never seen a clergywoman, though Lutherans began ordaining women in 1970. She felt like taking "a daring step of faith," preparing herself for something but she was not sure what. When she tentatively mentioned it to her parents, her father responded, "Oh, forget it," and returned to his newspaper. She remembers her mother in the kitchen murmuring, "Oh, my."

Christine attended Trinity Lutheran Seminary in Columbus, OH, a seminary of the American Lutheran Church, now the Evangelical Lutheran Church in America (ELCA). Her second master's degree was in theological studies, not in divinity as would be expected for her to be ordained.

While at Trinity Seminary she met Mark, who became her husband. They are both ordained Lutheran ministers and have been married more than thirty years. Christine laughs and says, "I followed Mark for the first ten years of our marriage. Now he follows me."

They knew Mark would likely find a job first, so Christine moved with him to Oshkosh, WI, where he became an assistant pastor of a very large Lutheran church. The congregation there voted to send her back to school, so she earned a master's degree in divinity from Wartburg Theological Seminary in Dubuque, IA, when their first child, a son, was just a baby. She became an assistant pastor in the same church where Mark was also an assistant pastor.

She laughs as she relates that she first served communion as an ordained pastor when she was eight months pregnant with their second child, a daughter, following her December ordination. She recalls that she filled out the vestments well and says, "What an Advent that was!" She also recalls that thirty-plus years ago there was no maternity leave so she took off four weeks without pay when her daughter was born.

The family moved to Albany, NY, when Mark became campus minister to Lutheran students at State University of New York at Albany. Christine served as associate pastor at a downtown Lutheran church. She wanted to go back to school but vowed, "I was not going to use household money" from their already-stretched budget. She scraped together almost $30,000 worth of grants and scholarships and enrolled at the Manhattan School of Music for her doctorate in musical arts, a performance degree in church music. During those years Christine played the organ at a church in nearby Schenectady. Mark arranged his schedule to care for their two young children while she was in Manhattan and somehow they managed until she received her degree.

An important part of Christine's religious development was staying with the Sisters of the Community of the Holy Spirit, a monastic order of nuns of the Episcopal Church located nine blocks from the Manhattan School of Music. While she worked on her degree, she stayed there a few days a week. She says, "They gave me my own cell."

The order practiced silence, even at mealtimes, and Christine says, "I discovered silence." She remembers that the two-hour train ride from New York City to Albany gave her time to transition to the noisy world and she was able to feel more available to her family when she arrived home. She later told the Mother Superior, "I'm not sure which was more important, living here or doing my degree." Christine later wrote an article called "A Season of Silence," and silence and meditation remain an important part of her spiritual life today.

"It almost felt like coming home [being in the silence of the community]," she remembers. "I didn't know how to find that in the Lutheran Church. It felt like I was home, almost a beginning. I didn't know how to harness that feeling."

Her first few calls had been part-time, but Christine accepted a job at Thiel College, a private liberal arts college in Greenville, PA, associated with the ELCA, and the family moved there. She was college pastor and also taught religion and music, since she was both an ordained minister and had the required academic credentials. She became tenured there before she left.

While she was working at Thiel College, her son joined the Civil Air Patrol (CAP). As a "'mom-thing'" she says with a laugh, Christine volunteered to be the chaplain for the squadron of cadets. She had to seek the endorsement of the ELCA in order to become the volunteer chaplain. She explains that each denomination has an "endorser," an official in the church charged with giving federal chaplains an endorsement to enter federal chaplaincy. She received the endorsement and set about the daunting task of teaching "moral leadership" to twelve- to eighteen-year-olds in the CAP. In return, she says, "The cadets taught me how to march and salute. I'm not typical military!"

The ELCA federal endorser asked her if she was interested in becoming an active duty military chaplain. "I was forty years old, tenured faculty. Previously I had looked into Army National Guard and Navy chaplaincy because I was curious. This needed to be a family decision. We sat at the dinner table and discussed it. My daughter said, 'We move every three or four years anyway. Why not?'"

Christine was forty-one years old when she was commissioned, first as a first lieutenant and then she entered the Air Force as a captain. Her federal endorser told her it was a thirty-six-month commitment and she could choose to separate from the military after that if she wanted to.

That was nineteen years ago and Christine is nearing the time when she can retire from the Air Force. She says, "I have now been in the military longer than I was a civilian pastor."

At the beginning, her mother was not so enthusiastic, however. She told Christine, dismayed, "I prayed you home." She asked Mark, "Can't you do something about your wife?" to which he replied, "You raised her!"

Thus began her military career. Christine believes the Biblical verse, "We walk by faith, not by sight," 2 Corinthians 5:7. "Very few chaplains come off the street into a direct commission. Most are prior military or have enlisted experience or were children of military," she says. "All I had was my father's long-ago World War II service. I was totally off the street." Her husband does not have military background, either.

So Christine made the transition from college professor and pastor to military chaplain. She says the first time she saw herself in battle dress, she laughed at her image in disbelief. "I was entering a new career at forty-one years old, a time when most people in the military retire."

Mark has adapted, finding work in the federal service as a civilian, serving as an interim minister on occasion. He jokes that he works mostly with women while Christine works mostly with men. He helps military personnel leaving the service to plan their finances as they enter civilian life.

She has had nine assignments in her nineteen years in the Air Force and has lived all over the world—Germany, Hawaii, Korea, including two tours in Iraq and one in Turkey—as well as stateside assignments. She has spent time at the Air University as a student at Air Command and Staff College and has taught at Chaplain School, as well as worked at the staff level for the Air Force chief of chaplains. She says her variety of assignments has helped develop her spirituality.

In many ways, being a military chaplain is like being a campus pastor, she says. "The age group is approximately the same milieu but the uniform is different. Young people have the same issues, aspirations and spiritual quests. The young people are no different in the military except they have chosen that career, have raised their right hands and sworn to protect the Constitution of the United States and now wear the uniform and share a common mission and commitment. You give up some freedoms but that frees you to serve.

"The beauty of the military chaplaincy is that you have ecclesiastic endorsement [from your denomination], fully a pastor yet fully an officer, too. You have two sets of rules, denominational and military."

Part of the chaplain's job is to ensure free expression of religion for everyone, regardless of faith or denomination, and to assist with accommodations for absolute freedom of religion. For example, Christine has helped establish a place for Buddhists to practice their chanting and helped Wiccans find a place to institute their circle, practice their rituals and study. All religious practices and protections on an air base are overseen by the chaplains on behalf of the commander, "including keeping one group from denigrating another. The key is showing respect and honoring all."

The Chaplain Corps includes chaplains, enlisted assistants, and usually contracted musicians, religious education directors and worship coordinators. Work of the chaplain service includes conducting worship, counseling, visitation in units and even on the flight line (where planes land and take off). Chaplains are noncombatants and do not carry arms; chaplain's assistants are combatants and do carry arms. Usually in a combat area, they travel as a team, affording some protection for the chaplains.

Christine says it's important to maintain objectivity and an inclusive manner toward those who believe differently. She has worked with chaplains and assistants from many denominations that do not ordain women. She maintains her own liberal views but insists that others who work with her have equal right to their own more conservative beliefs. She has worked with a wide range of Christian and non-Christian faith leaders throughout her military career.

She has advanced from her initial entry rank of captain to her present rank of lieutenant colonel. "In the Air Force, chaplains' official title is chaplain, not their military rank. We are also permitted to be called pastor, father, rabbi, etc., according to our faith tradition. I have had some folks call me Chaplain Christine. Most call me Chaplain Blice-Baum or Chaplain BB for short. We generally do not use first names—I never do. I joke that my first name is 'Chaplain.'"

She wears all-purpose battle uniform—ABUs—to work most days. The general public might call them camis, the grayish-sandy desert-pattern military fatigues most generally seen these days. For special occasions she wears service dress, a more formal uniform.

"Over the years when I do services—I don't do that much now that I am at a higher rank because I oversee everything—I wear my typical liturgical garb—alb, stole, chasuble over a suit with a clerical collar. In the deployed setting, I always wore the same robes but over the ABUs. I usually led a liturgical service, serving mostly Lutherans, Episcopalians and more mainline folks. The worshipping communities (we don't call them congregations) consisted of active duty and families, retired military, and overseas civilians."

There are currently two Lutheran women serving as Air Force Chaplains, about five percent of the total chaplain force. She says the military chaplaincy is the first time she has received pay equal with men in her profession.

"Chaplains serve at the base level as duty chaplain," says

Christine, "which means the Command Post will call them after hours for all base-wide emergencies or when someone wants to speak with a chaplain. Most chaplains are duty chaplain for a week at a time. As the wing chaplain, I generally do not answer after-hour emergency calls but will go when needed. Our 'congregation' is the entire base! The base-level chaplains serve as part of disaster teams. Chaplains are trained to accompany commanders when we have to do death notifications to next of kin."

All chaplains and chaplain assistants have to do readiness training and be prepared for deployments and contingency operations at all times. "I feel the training is excellent for everyday life," she says. "We are taught situational awareness that I did not have as a civilian pastor. We are always 'on,' even when on leave. We consider what we do twenty-four/seven. I remind my staff that we always represent the Chaplain Corps and that our actions reflect our vocation and calling. My staff salutes me when they meet me outside. I consider it an honor to return the salute!"

Throughout her nonmilitary and military careers, Christine says though her faith has changed, she herself has never experienced a personal crisis in her faith. She has evolved in her spiritual beliefs over time. "I've become more introspective, moved from believing and belonging to loving and living, more contemplative and meditative, moving from head knowledge to heart knowledge."

She has become interested in the Taizé Community in France and has visited there. This ecumenical movement offers silence and meditative singing as a means of worship, not talking but experiencing. Christine practices mindfulness meditation and is receiving her training in mindfulness-based stress reduction.. She is also a certified yoga and mindfulness instructor. She began doing yoga with a group of women while she was in Iraq and believes Christian meditation and silence may be a part of the next phase of her life and work.

She says, "When I go into a silent retreat, it's a different world, no electronic devices."

Christine advises women considering the clergy to "be secure in who they are. Also be curious, willing to learn and grow. In our vocation, as the Spirit moves, so will we change and grow." She grins and adds, "And have fun!"

She talks about the religious thinkers who have influenced her development—Richard Rohr, Thomas Keating, Cynthia Bourgeault, Jack Kornfield and Donald Rothbert—especially in the areas of mindfulness and meditation.

She contemplates her future as she retires from the military. Her two adult children are both scientists, though born of non-scientific parents, and she has no grandchildren, so she and Mark can choose wherever they want to live. They are building a retirement house in Ponte Vedra, FL, and plan to use it as a second home until they retire. Christine hopes to lead meditation groups in Florida in retirement, helping others find their own spirituality through meditation and yoga.

"Or maybe I'll write books ..." She has one publication listed on Amazon, a paper she wrote for Air Command and Staff College, on psychological effects of bombing in World War II, *O Day of Wrath: A Case Study in Collateral Damage and Psychological Effects*, and has published several articles on various topics. Clearly her future will be active, evolving, and full of curiosity as well as spirituality as she develops her post-retirement life's work.

CHAPTER 19
Amy

AMY PORTERFIELD TURNER, THIRTY-THREE, was ordained as an Episcopal priest five years ago.

Amy arrives at the interview saying, "I just got off the phone from an interview for a chaplaincy in a school, my passion, my dream. Pastoral ministry is not where my heart is. I want to teach and be in a school during the week."

Currently Amy is in a school all week, but in a secular setting, teaching Latin to high school students in a public school. While she enjoys the job, her dream is to be a chaplain in a denominational school where she teaches and leads worship as well. She says with a laugh, "My students now don't even know I'm a priest." However, she sees this time as preparation for the school chaplaincy she hopes will materialize one day very soon.

She is a tall, self-possessed young woman, with shoulder-length brown hair and a dressy print dress with short flared sleeves. Her earrings and necklace are in a Celtic design of Trinity knots, and her wedding rings echo this motif. She is headed to a long Maundy Thursday service following this interview, after a full day of teaching, yet gives her complete attention to the interviewer and speaks fluently and candidly.

Growing up in Charles Town, WV, a fifth-generation Episcopalian and the descendant of a prominent American Revolutionary War figure, Amy labels herself as "cradle-plus" in the denomination. Her family was active in the church, with both her parents serving on the vestry (elected governing body) of their parish. Her father served as chalice bearer and lector while she was growing up, and she recalls accompanying him to the eight a.m. service and sitting in the front pew when he was participating in leading the service. She laughs and says, "I'm one of the few priests who actually prefers the Rite One [traditionally offered for older parishioners at an early-morning service] instead of Rite Two."

She attended Bible school at her church and when she grew out of class age, became a Bible school helper. Church summer camp at Peterkin Camp at Romney, WV, was a highlight of her life and she continued with that through becoming a camp counselor. She got to know some female priests at camp, though there was not a clergywoman at her own church while she was growing up.

Her middle school years were not the best time in her life. She grew up with an older brother who had special needs and her mother, a psychologist, became a stay-at-home mother to take care of her children. Amy remembers, "They [school personnel] pulled me out of class and lunch to help calm him down when my brother had an outburst."

Her parents had always been careful to ensure that Amy was not thrust into a parental role with her brother, so this change in her life during middle school gave her a feeling of responsibility that was perhaps inappropriate at her young age. That, coupled with a perceived lack of academic rigor at the public high school she was headed for—Amy was in the gifted program in middle school—engendered a family decision to send her to a private boarding school for her high school years.

She attended and loved St. Timothy's in Stephenson, MD, outside Baltimore, a well-recognized all-girls Episcopal school. The school emphasizes both academics and athletics, and counts among its alumnae Kimberly Dozier, a CBS reporter who was critically wounded in the Iraq War; Liz Claiborne, fashion designer; and Mary Pillsbury Lord, former U.S. delegate to the United Nations General Assembly.

At St. Timothy's, Amy met Rev. Bob Miller, the school chaplain, whose daughters attended the school. A school chaplain leads worship, teaches religious courses, does pastoral care of students and staff, and serves as the religious voice of the school. The chaplain ensures that religion is at the heart of conversations, whether it be a denominationally-affiliated school or secular.

Amy realized she might someday be ordained and become a priest like Rev. Bob. She sees this as the genesis of her goal to become a school chaplain. "I think it was there, though I was not aware of it. I can look back and see all the pieces leading up to it [her dream]."

She attended Washington University in St. Louis. "I wanted a small, academically strong school," she says. Academically strong it is, with schools of business, engineering, law, medicine, design, social work and public health, and arts and sciences. One inviting aspect of the matriculation process was a summer phone call from an Episcopalian student, welcoming her to the school. She enrolled as an engineering student but that lasted only a semester. She thought about special education law but ended up taking majors in religious studies and in the classics, having enjoyed her study of Latin in high school.

"I didn't know what I was missing until I went to college," Amy recalls. "A lot of my spiritual formation had been in camp and Christian education classes. These form you into a stronger Christian." When she arrived at Washington University, "I went to five-thirty service, which is what the college students attended. I got so involved, my classmates teased me, saying I was always in church and maybe over-involved. I took my first religious studies class."

She says, "I grew into it. There was no real 'aha moment' when I named it. I became aware, 'Is this what I'm called to be?'" She still recalls "the scariness of the magnitude of that awareness."

A semester of study abroad in Australia provided "pivotal awareness" for Amy. She had been dating someone in college ministry and had "a bad break-up, not healthy. A lot of my friendships were through him. I had to discover who I was when I was alone. Most people had known us as a couple." The semester abroad "felt free. I learned who I am, I felt free."

She remembers sneaking into a Roman Catholic service to get ashes on Ash Wednesday—"Easter is in the fall there. It was a tiny little church. I was in Australia doing research for my marine biology class. The people in the church wanted me to read at Easter, a visiting American." She felt free, valued and validated there.

She returned from Australia with the decision to pursue a master's degree in theological studies. She knew she wanted to go to graduate school to study religion in the fall but had nothing lined up for the summer. She returned to her childhood Peterkin Camp, "a place dear and special to my heart." She climbed up to the outdoor chapel, Prayer Hill, a space "up a hill in the woods, maintained by the youth with wooden pews." There Amy had the distinct feeling that God spoke to her. "I heard the words in my head, 'Why are you limiting me?'"

She had previously thought she might serve the church as a teacher or something, but from these words she sensed that she might not have set her sights high enough. "I wasn't sure what the words meant. It was a scary event." She laughs and adds parenthetically, "It amuses me in religion, you hear voices and no one ever bats an eye!"

The bishop was visiting and she talked with him. He told her she needed to do discernment within her parish and said, "Talk to me when you have more clarity."

She talked to her parish priest, who said, "Have you ever seen yourself behind the altar lifting up the bread and wine?"

Amy replied, "I think so."

The priest said, "We need to get you into the discernment process." The Episcopal church requires this process to determine if the interested person does indeed have a calling to the deaconate or the priesthood. Amy's home parish ultimately became her sponsoring parish.

"I knew this would take awhile," she says. She began the process near the end of her senior year in college and continued it into her next year, which she spent with the Episcopal Service Corps in Philadelphia, a group of recent college graduates doing a servant year after graduation.

The summer between college and her next year in Philadelphia "was a tough summer for a variety of reasons." She was the head counselor that summer at Peterkin Camp and encountered some difficult situations. She saw disputes among people about how to handle these situations "and saw the uglier side of it, of ministry and humanity. I thought, 'I'm going to be a priest and be a part of this?'" She told her discernment committee, "I don't want to be a priest, no more discernment."

She says now, "I was probably depressed, just reeling from the ugliness." However, by the end of the summer, "I got back together, sorted through this, decided I didn't hate God," she says. "Another counselor helped me tremendously. I started going to church and being a part of it every day. The process of being in it worked."

She left camp to attend the annual conference and in the middle of the night, preparatory to leaving the next morning, had "another God-moment, whether auditory or voices, who knows?" She heard, "Whenever you stop running, I'll be waiting for you, I'm here."

Amy went back to her discernment committee and said, "Let's start again," to which they responded, "Let's do it over." She said, "They treated me like a pause in the middle. There were so many changes. They said, 'Let's start in a few months.' So we began again, at a much deeper place because I was more aware. I saw that I had grown, felt I had shattered, hadn't known what to do besides run away. The pieces came out in a richer pattern. I know I've had situational depression at various points."

She went on to her servant year in Philadelphia. The website of the sponsoring organization (www.episcopalservicecorps.org), says, "The Episcopal Service Corps invites men and women in their twenties to work for justice, live in Christian community, grown in leadership, and deepen their faith life."

Amy's assignment was Project HOME in Philadelphia, an organization working with the homeless with the motto, "None of us are home until all of us are home." Founded by Sister Mary Scullion, a member of the order of Sisters of Mercy, the group provides after-school care, street outreach, and other services to the homeless population of Philadelphia.

"What a change, from a small town, a sheltered campus, to do a census count of the homeless on a street in Philadelphia at two a.m.!" recalls Amy. "It made me connect more with Jesus. I'd felt a connection with God the Father and God the Holy Spirit previously, as a good father image and then the Holy Spirit. But I felt Jesus' presence, His hands in the world, as my eyes opened to center city Philadelphia. It was great but challenging. I was so glad to do it. It was important in my discernment process."

After her year in Philadelphia, Amy enrolled at Virginia Theological Seminary (VTS) in Alexandria, where she received her master of divinity degree. "VTS was known for commitment and producing good parish priests and had a larger young population. I was the fifth youngest in my class, thirty students, which included twelve women."

There she met her husband, Brian Turner, a fellow class member, now also a priest. "We were in all the same classes." Amy says a small group of five emerged as a support system. "We are still in touch, still best friends," and she is headed off soon to visit one who has moved to California.

When Amy and Brian were ordained, her mother made them red stoles embroidered with the holy images of a dove and flames. Their stoles are mirror images: Amy's also has an A on the back and Brian's, a B. Sometimes when they celebrate the Holy Eucharist, they wear their stoles.

The newly ordained couple agreed that whoever received a solid offer first, the other would follow. Brian received and accepted a call as associate pastor and campus minister at Trinity Episcopal Church in Fredericksburg, VA. So they moved and Brian became a campus minister / parish priest while Amy accepted employment as hospital chaplain at Mary Washington Hospital—not her dream job as a school chaplain.

Realistically she knows that there are few positions as school chaplains but even so, the move to Fredericksburg was difficult for her. "I sat on the back pew and felt depressed, watching him celebrate the Eucharist," she recalls.

"So here I was. I was taught to be wonderful and I hitched my wagon to my husband and here I am." While she enjoyed some aspects of her chaplaincy at the hospital and she felt very capable there, she didn't think that advanced her toward her goal as a school chaplain. "I think of it as my desert time period, being in the wilderness."

Amy is in her fourth year now as a Latin teacher in a public high school. She has earned a master's degree in education from Mary Washington University to attain her teaching credentials. "It's been good. My students don't know I'm a priest. I do a lot of pastoral care incognito, checking in on them." Amy gives the example of a student failing to turn in homework because a grandparent had died, and she's concerned about the student's reaction to the grief more than the missed homework assignment. She believes this experience teaching in the public schools will serve her well when she attains her goal of being a school chaplain. "I should know the education piece as well as the religious part. I'll fit into the faculty better."

At this point in her life, she says, "I'm just happy to be teaching. But I want to be all I can be. I'm not hiding that I'm ordained, but not fully displaying it." She does a lot of supply work, filling in for other priests on the weekends, "feeding my spiritual and sacramental needs." She is preaching or assisting someone most weekends this spring.

Regarding interviews for school chaplain positions, she says,

"I keep on being runner-up, runner-up. I'm hoping this is the year." Currently her life as a priest and a teacher, she sums up with, "It's tough but good. Lots of rough patches that lead up to amazing moments."

Her advice to other young women considering the ministry: "It's not easy but it's rewarding."

CHAPTER 20
Amazing Women!

EVERY ONE OF THE amazing women I asked to interview agreed, busy though they all were. What I've learned from these women is also amazing. While they are all different, they also have some common characteristics. Their lives and careers have taken a different path than mine, but I found many similarities with my own experiences. Even some coincidences emerged: one woman's father and my mother both grew up in the same very small town in Missouri!

    I interviewed women in their own homes and offices, in my home and in the living room of mutual friends, and most often in coffee shops. Clergywomen really like coffee! We met in three different branches of the Front Porch Coffee Shop at Outer Banks, a coffee shop at St. Simons Island, and Blackstone Coffee in Fredericksburg. The women—and the coffee shops—were uniformly gracious and welcoming to me. Every clergywoman possessed a vibrancy and a passion for what they were doing, as I expected to find. Their differences were not as wide as I'd anticipated, but maybe that was to be expected, given that many of them share common beliefs and have similar preparation for their jobs.

The most surprising fact to me was that not one of the clergywomen had known a female pastor in her own church as she was growing up, though some of their denominations ordained women at that time. I watched a four-year-old boy in my own church a few Sundays ago sitting rapt as the priest stood in the middle of the aisle and read us the Gospel for the day. The child appeared to be spellbound and, with my head in this *Voices* book instead of the one the Gospel came from, I idly wondered if that little boy might be visualizing himself in that role one day.

It then dawned on me that none of the women who became pastors or chaplains had had that experience as children. They never gazed at a woman preaching to them in their own church. I am glad that the little girls in my congregation see women priests, and also women bishops. Times do change, if slowly sometimes.

The three Roman Catholic sisters in the book did know sisters as they grew up; they had all been taught by them. The three in this book also had family members who had taken holy orders. Some of their brothers and uncles became priests; some of their aunts and sisters, members of women's religious orders, sometimes the same order they themselves later chose.

The women are a very well-educated group; several of the women attended private high schools. Almost all hold a master's degree (some with two or more), two have post-master's educational specialist degrees, and five hold doctorates. Many of their degrees are not in divinity; some are in mental health, nursing, social work, law, music and administration. In most instances they did not go directly into a graduate program from their undergraduate degrees, but waited some years until their career paths had consolidated to pursue graduate studies.

Fourteen of the nineteen women attended traditional seminary programs—Southern Baptist, Presbyterian, Episcopal, Lutheran, Methodist, United Church of Christ and the three sisters all received extensive education within their orders. Some of the women attended non-denominational Christian seminaries. One white woman attended a historically black seminary. One black woman attended what appears to be from the website to be a predominantly white seminary. The woman who pastors the largest church in this book has not been to any seminary but has advanced degrees in other disciplines. Some of the women attended seminaries of denominations other than those they ended up serving.

The names of some colleges and universities popped up more than once. Two women have graduate degrees from George Mason University, neither in a religious field. Wesley Seminary emerged a few times. At least three women were involved with the Shalem Institute. The similarities would have been less startling if the women had been of the same denomination, but they were not, though geography was probably a factor in where the women studied.

I found it interesting that several women—almost half, in fact—had either changed denominations or had early influence from a different denomination than the one that ultimately ordained them. Four of the nineteen began their lives as Roman Catholics, with others having significant influence from that background, as well. As they chronicled their faith journeys to me in the interviews, it was fascinating to see how much we are one, regardless of where we start. Many of the women interviewed talked about their ties to and work with other denominations. Three of the women left their own denominations—or branches of their denominations—as a result of their wish to become ordained ministers in a milieu that did not support women's ordination.

Some new words emerged, not exactly buzz words but rather words that clergy commonly use these days. Some women used "call" to mean God's voice; others, an offer from a church to work there. I frequently heard the words emergent, contemplative, discernment, ecumenical, charismatic, spiritual formation and apostolic. I heard about "God moments" and "God-cidents." I heard stories that validated what I'd read in Christine Smith's *Beyond the Stained Glass Ceiling* and Sarah Sentilles' *A Church of Her Own: What Happens When a Woman Takes the Pulpit*.

Most of the women had family members who participated in church life. All three of the Roman Catholic sisters had close family who took holy orders. Some of the others had clergy in their families—all men, fathers or grandfathers or brothers. Most came from families that attended church regularly, though a few did not and became acquainted with church through grandparents. Five of the women in the book are married to clergymen. Some of the women's husbands and children are employed with them in their ministries or in charities related to their ministries. One co-pastors a church with her husband currently. I think an interesting later book might be *Couples of the Cloth*.

Of the fourteen women who are or have been married, seven revealed they have been divorced. With the American divorce rate somewhere between forty and fifty percent, according to the American Psychological Association (www.apa.org/topics/divorce), this rate for the clergywomen is on the higher side. However—and I have been divorced myself—these are women who could afford to leave a marriage, as they were or would become self-supporting. All but one (who is not married now) are currently in a second marriage of many years, even though the divorce rate for second marriages, according to APA, is even higher.

Six of the women alluded to depression or other mental health issues they'd experienced, though all of these conversations did not end up in the book. Some talked about the benefits they had gained from going to counseling themselves. Others described periods in their lives when someone probably would have diagnosed depression if they'd sought help. It is difficult to find a good estimate of depression, but the National Institute of Mental Health (www.nimh.nih.gov/health/topics/depression) estimates that almost seven percent of Americans suffered a major depressive episode in 2014. However, the Depression and Bipolar Support Alliance (www.dbsalliance.org) estimates twenty to twenty-six percent of women will at some time suffer from depression.

The number who discussed depression is higher among these women than in the American population in general, but perhaps not surprising. These women are well-educated and introspective enough to realize when they needed help, and open enough to talk about it. They are likely associated with colleagues or mentors who might recognize the need for mental health assistance. Three of them are licensed mental health professionals themselves, as am I.

The interesting part of this: it was not a question on the interview guide I used, nor did I ever ask anyone about her own mental health. It was a part of the women's stories that emerged through conversation, with no attempt on my part to elicit the information. Often their decision to enter the ministry evolved after a period of bleakness in their own lives.

The facts they gave me about their lives in many instances paralleled what the few research studies on women clergy show. As cited in the first chapter of this book, women often are employed in smaller churches, chaplaincies, part-time positions or interim positions. Only two of the nineteen women in the book are senior pastors in large churches, though the military chaplain holds a position that would be equivalent. Five others are or have been solo pastors of a smaller church. One woman serves two churches together; two others are or have been interim ministers.

The primary work of several of the women has not been work within a church but rather in community centers, schools, the military, or hospitals or other nursing facilities. At least six have been designated chaplains in an organization. Two have become entrepreneurial with their own businesses related to the ministry.

Many of the women became clergy after having other well-established careers, attending seminary as mid-life career changes. They first held jobs as teacher, Christian educator, nurse, lawyer, social worker, Congressional aide, counselor, journalist, and librarian. Only five of the women—including all three of the younger women in the book—went directly into religious work or study without having had significant time in other careers first, and one of them took a time-out for a few years.

Several of the women made career concessions that deferred to their roles as family members—spouses, mothers, daughters. Some had husbands who did not want them to become clergy, though eventually they became great supporters of their wives. Others did not pursue the churches they might have because family members required more-than-usual time, or frequent or geographic moves might have been detrimental to the family or a family member. Some chose whether or not to be ordained or what kind of ordination to seek based on family considerations. Those of us who are mothers, partners, and daughters are familiar with balancing family needs against career needs.

I myself completed my doctorate when my three children were young, with a huge amount of support from their father, so I can understand their career decisions. Some mentioned the positive influence of their children seeing them in seminary pursuing a graduate degree and a career goal. They believe, as my children tell me was true for them, that seeing their mother work so hard toward a dream was beneficial to their own career achievements.

The women have advice and suggestions for other women thinking about entering the clergy. They insist the woman pray and be very sure of her calling before she embarks on the arduous journey to get there. They tell her to be aware of economic realities but to understand her own worth and not settle for a lower salary because she is a woman; three of the women in the book revealed that they received lower compensation than the men they replaced. She may find more parity in denominations where women's ordination is more established.

She will need a support group for the hard times—many of these women found theirs in the women and men with whom they attended seminary, and their professors there. She will need to continue her own spiritual growth and worship, even when the demands of her job seem overwhelming. They advise that the ability to multi-task will serve her well and that she will need strong interpersonal skills. There will be dark days but she should persevere through them to achieve her calling, and expect spiritual growth from these dark days.

They advise her that she will not feel satisfied with her life if she ignores the voice from God. She may decide to become a chaplain, associate pastor, a pastor in a small church or an interim minister as she works her way into her chosen field. Or one of these positions may be her final goal.

Some changes have occurred in these women's lives since the interviews were completed in 2015 or in the early months of 2016. One has lost a parent; another has gained a grandchild—and she did baptize that grandchild. One has retired, two others are contemplating retirement, and one is trying hard not to be retired. One has accepted an interim position in Hawaii. Another has been granted a sabbatical to care for an ailing family member. At least three have been seeking other jobs, and one of them has received the offer she has dreamed of. Two have taken teaching jobs and are thrilled to be beginning them in the fall of 2016. Two are dealing with serious health issues of their spouses and one is fighting a recurrence of cancer. One has received a significant promotion in her job responsibilities.

A final thought I carried away from the interviews is that I have been talking to happy women who have found satisfaction in the career paths they chose. They believe they made good decisions and fulfilled their need to make this world a better place. Not one expressed regret at her career choice, though some cautioned that women (or men, for that matter) considering the clergy must be very aware of the economic realities they may face in today's clergy employment.

I would personally feel comfortable confiding in any of the women I talked to as a religious guide. I felt the sincerity of each and every one, and would probably enjoy the church service any would lead, although admittedly one or two might be pretty foreign to my usual Episcopal order of worship.

Thanks be to God for these amazing women!

APPENDIX A
Denominational Ordination of Women

DENOMINATIONS THAT ORDAIN WOMEN PASTORS
American Baptist Church
Buddhist
Episcopal Church
Evangelical Lutheran Church in America
Jewish (Reform and Conservative Movements)
Presbyterian Church (USA)
United Church of Christ, Unitarian Universalist
United Methodist Church
Pentecostal Church of God
Assemblies of God
African Methodist Episcopal
Disciples of Christ
Christian Science

DENOMINATIONS THAT DO NOT GENERALLY ORDAIN WOMEN AS PASTORS
Jewish Orthodox
Latter Day Saints (Mormon)

Missouri Synod Lutheran Church
Muslim
Orthodox Church in American
Southern Baptist Convention
Roman Catholic Church

Source: Kuruvilla, Carol (2014). These are the religious denominations that ordain women. Huffington Post, 9/26/14. www.huffingtonpost.com/2014/09/26/religion-ordain-women_n_5826422.html.

APPENDIX B
Denominational Ordination History

American Baptist Church—The first Baptist clergywoman was ordained in the 1800s. By 1985, three percent of senior pastors and sixteen percent of assistant/associate pastors were women. By 2002, fourteen percent of all ordained ABC ministers were women; eight percent of senior pastors were women and thirty-three percent of associate/assistant pastors were clergywomen (Adams, 2010).

The ABC (American Baptist Church) Female Pastor Study (2009-2011) showed that women's age at first pastorate was usually between forty and forty-nine, and about two-thirds of the women identified as Anglo-American. About sixty percent of the women were employed for thirty or more hours a week and two-thirds of them were married. The average age of clergywomen responding to the survey was fifty-six or older and the average congregation size was fifty to one hundred (Smith, 2013).

The Southern Baptist Convention, according to the website (www.sbc.net/faqs), does not endorse women as pastors but an individual congregation can ordain a woman if it chooses to. The first female Southern Baptist pastor was ordained in 1964 by a congregation in North Carolina (Adams, 2010). Melva

(Chapter 3) graduated from a Southern Baptist seminary and Donna (Chapter 14) is a Baptist Elder.

Episcopal Church—Researchers in a 2008 study who interviewed female Episcopal priests showed that most knew from childhood that they wanted to be employed by the church but most knew no female ministers when they were growing up (Sentilles, 2008). The ordination of the first eleven Episcopal women priests in 1974 and the ordination of the next four in 1975 were declared "irregular" and "invalid" by the church. However, in 1976, church leaders yielded to pressure and allowed women to be ordained as priests and "regularized" the previous fifteen ordinations.

Almost half of all candidates for ordination to priesthood now are women and currently about one-third of Episcopal priests are women. However, males still predominate in higher levels of leadership, though the past-presiding bishop of the denomination is a woman. For example, most bishops and cathedral deans are currently male (Tammeus, 2014). Pam (Chapter 2), Torrence (Chapter 8) and Amy (Chapter 19) are Episcopal priests. Tanya (Chapter 9) has been affiliated with the Episcopal denomination as has Margaret (Chapter 12).

Lutheran—The branches of the Lutheran Church that became the Evangelical Lutheran Church of America (ELCA) began ordaining women as ministers in 1970. In 2013 a woman was elected presiding bishop of ELCA, the highest position in the church (ELCA, 2015). Women are not ordained as pastors in the Lutheran Church-Missouri Synod, citing Biblical New Testament statements in Corinthians and Timothy as reasons for ordaining men only (LCMS, 2015). Sarah (Chapter 6), Kate (Chapter 13) and Christine (Chapter 18) are ordained Lutheran pastors.

Methodist—Women were awarded full clergy rights by the vote of the 1956 General Conference of the United Methodist Church, although women preachers in this denomination date back to John Wesley licensing women to preach, beginning in 1761 in England. Most clergywomen in the UMC are in churches, though women are more likely to leave congregations for other ministry than are clergymen, citing lack of support by leadership of the church. About ninety-five percent of the women are in local churches; ninety-eight percent of African-American women and almost one hundred percent of Asian-American women pastors serve local churches.

There is still discrepancy in the areas of job security, opportunities to lead larger congregations, and commensurate salaries, many believe (Burton, 2014). In 2009 there were around 10,000 clergywomen in the UMW, about twenty-three percent of the denomination's clergy. However, only eighty-five women served the largest churches, compared to 1,082 men (French, 2009). Brenda (Chapter 7) and Betsy (Chapter 16) are clergy in the United Methodist Church.

Nazarene—The Church of the Nazarene has ordained women as evangelists and pastors, as well as to other leadership positions in the denomination, since its inception in 1908 (Houseal, 2003). The denomination cites Acts 2:17, "Your sons and your daughters shall prophesy," as authority for ordaining women. The number and percentage of clergywomen compared to clergymen peaked in 1955 and has declined somewhat since then. Women represented almost eleven percent of all Nazarene clergy in 2003 but were just under four percent of pastors, often serving in smaller churches. Almost twenty-five percent of female clergy were unassigned in 2003, compared to seventeen percent of unassigned male clergy. Dr. Carla D. Sunberg was chosen as president of Nazarene Theological Seminary in 2014 (Wesleyan/Holiness Women Clergy). Gaye (Chapter 10) is associated with the Nazarene denomination.

Presbyterian—The Presbyterian USA church approved ordination of women in 1956; the Presbyterian Church US (primarily Southern) followed in 1964. However, at least some of the early women to be ordained were in Christian education, not bound for pulpits. There were dramatic gains in the 1990s in the numbers of women ordained, although they had begun entering seminary in larger numbers beginning in the 1960s in this denomination (Boyd & Brackenridge, 1996).

According to the National Association of Presbyterian Clergywomen, there are more women than men chaplains, but men outnumber women about two to one in other clergy categories. There are fewer solo clergywomen and most women pastor smaller congregations. Very few of the largest churches have female ministers (NAPC, 2014). There are relatively few African-American Presbyterian clergywomen (Brown & Felton, 2001). There is an organization called the Korean-American Presbyterian Clergywomen. Some branches of the Presbyterian Church (Associate Reformed Presbyterian Church, Bible Presbyterian Church, Presbyterian Reformed Church, and others) do not ordain women as ministers (Christians for Biblical Equality [CBE], 2007). Jann (Chapter 11) is a minister in the Presbyterian Church USA.

Roman Catholic—Women serve in the Roman Catholic Church worldwide, as nuns who live a contemplative life in a monastery, usually cloistered or semi-cloistered, or as sisters who live, minister and pray as "active" or "apostolic" members serving within the world. Both groups take vows of poverty, celibacy and obedience and both are addressed as "sister." (www.anunslife. org/resources/sister-or-nun) The number of Roman Catholic sisters in America peaked in 1965 at 180,000; in 2010 there were 56,000 sisters (McGuinness, 2013). Michele and Monique (Chapter 4) and Sister Miriam Elizabeth (Chapter 17) are Roman Catholic sisters.

The Roman Catholic church does not ordain women as priests. In 1994 Pope John Paul II reinforced that traditional belief, saying, "I declare that the church has no authority whatsoever to confer priestly ordination on women and that this judgment is to be definitely held by all the church's faithful." (www.catholic.com/tracts/women-and-the-priesthood) Pope Francis more recently reiterated, "With regards to the ordination of women, the church has spoken and says no ... that door is closed." (www.ncronline.org/blogs/ncr-today/pope-francis-and-womens-ordination)

However, there are active women priests in America and elsewhere in the world, according to the website of Roman Catholic Womenpriests, an organization dedicated to the ordination of women (www.romancatholicwomenpriests.org/interationalmovement). The website states, "The mission of the international RCWP movement is to prepare, ordain in apostolic succession and support primarily women who are called to the priesthood in an inclusive church." According to the website, they consider themselves in "Apostolic Succession" because their women bishops were ordained by Roman Catholic male bishops. There are ordained women priests in over thirty-two states and the website lists locations by state of congregations with women priests. A 2010 poll by the *New York Times* and CBS found that fifty-nine percent of American Catholics favor ordination of women as priests (Levitt, 2012).

United Church of Christ—The first woman ordained in America in a major Protestant denomination was Antoinette L. Brown in the Congregationalist church, which became a part of the United Church of Christ (UCC), in upstate New York in 1853 (Zikmund, Lummis, and Chang, 1998). The Antoinette Brown Award is given today by the UCC "celebrating the life and ministry of the first woman ordained into Christian ministry since biblical times..." (www.ucc.org/women). There are many women in the UCC ministerial ranks now, and the denomination trailed only the Methodists in percent of female clergy in 1998 (Zikmund, Lummis and Chang, 1998). A 2002 study (Lehman) showed approximately twenty-five percent of UCC ministers were women. Cathie (Chapter 5) and Mary (Chapter 15) are ordained in the UCC church.

Unitarian—The Unitarian Universalist Association (UUA) had its first clergywoman in 1863 when the Universalists ordained Olympia Brown (Unitarian Universalists Association, no date). The UU churches were early supporters of women's rights, including ordination of women. As late as the late 1970s, women represented only about five percent of clergy in the UU. The Women and Religion Resolution was passed by the General Assembly in 1977, leading to the feminization of God in language and song in worship (Owen-Towle, 2011). Issues of human rights came to the forefront in the church. In 2007, about fifty-three percent of active UU ministers were women, the first denomination with more than half its clergy to be female (Paulson, 2007). Margaret (Chapter 12) is a clergywoman of this denomination.

Sources Cited or Consulted

Adams, Sheri (2010). Myth: Baptists don't believe in women pastors. *Christian Ethics Today*, December 27, 2010. www.christianethicstoday.com.

Bailey, Judith Anne Bledsoe (2015). *Strength for the journey: Feminist theology and Baptist women pastors.* Richmond, VA: Center for Baptist Heritage and Studies.

Bethany Community Faith Statements (1974, 1985).

Boyd, Lois A. and Brackenridge, R. Douglas. (1996). *Presbyterian women in America: Two centuries of a quest for status* (2nd Ed.). Westport, CT: Greenwood Press.

Brown, Karen V. & Felton, Phyllis M. (2001). *African-American Presbyterian clergywomen: The first 25 years.* Louisville, KY: Witherspoon Press.

Burton, M. Garlinda (2014). Women pastors growing in numbers. *United Methodist News*, www.umc.org/news-and-media/women-pastors-growing-in-numbers, March 20, 2014.

Busey, Jane. Is the glass ceiling cracking? National Association of Presbyterian Clergywomen. *Connections*, Spring 2014, p. 8.

Carroll, Jackson W., Hargrove, Barbara, and Lummus, Adair T. (1983). *Women of the cloth: A new opportunity for the churches.* San Francisco: Harper and Row.

Christians for Biblical Equality (CBE) International. US denominations and their stances on women in leadership. E-Quality, 6 (2), www.e-quality.cbeinterational.org.

Church Women United (2015). www.churchwomen.org.

Encyclopedia Britannica, www.britannica.com/biography/Anne-Hutchinson.

Episcopal Church Home Website. www.episcopalchurch.org/page/katharine-jefferts-schori-biography. Accessed 3/23/15

Evangelical Lutheran Church in America. News and Events, 2015. www.elca.org/news-and-events/ELCA-facts.

French, Rose (2009). Methodist women seek to pastor large churches. The Christian Post, www.christianpost.com/news/methodist-women-seek-to-pastor-large-churches-36535, January 21, 2009.

Grossman, Cathy Lynn. US churches feel beat of change: More diversity, more drums. Religion News Service, September 11, 2014. www.religionnews.com/2014/09/11/2014/churches-change-evangelical-catholic.

Hamm, Thomas D. (2003). *The Quakers in America*. New York: Columbia University Press.

Hein, Avi. Women in Judaism: A history of women's ordination as rabbis. Jewish Virtual Library. www.jewishvirtuallibrary.org. Accessed 8/4/15.

Houseal, Richard W., Jr. Women Clergy in the Church of the Nazarene: An Analysis of Change from 1908-1995. M.S. Thesis, University of Missouri-Kansas City, 1996.

Houseal, Richard. Nazarene clergy women: A statistical analysis from 1908 to 2003. www.nazarene.org/files/docs/houseal_03.pdf.

Journal of Lutheran Ethics, March 3, 2016 issue.

Keller, Rosemary Skinner & Ruether, Rosemary Radford, eds., with Cantlon, Marie, Associate Editor (2006). *Encyclopedia of women and religion in North America*. Bloomington, IN: Indiana University Press.

Kidd, Sue Monk. (2014). *The invention of wings*. New York: Viking Penguin.

Kuruvilla, Carol (2014). These are the religious denominations that ordain women. Huffington Post, 9/26/14. www.huffingtonpost.com/2014/09/26/religion-ordain-women_n_5826422.html.

Lehman, Edward C., Jr. (2002). Women's Path into Ministry: Six Major Studies. Pulpit & Pew Research Reports (No.

1, Fall 2002). Durham, NC: Duke Divinity School. www.pulpitandpew.duke.

Levitt, Judith (2012). http://www.nytimes.com/2012/09/30/opinion/sunday/women-as-priests.html?

Lizardy-Jajbi, Kristina (2014). https://carducc.wordpress.com/2014/04/06/statistics-on-ucc-female-ministers.

Lutheran Church – Missouri Synod. "Faqs." www.lcms.org/faqs/worship. 2015. The web site gives facts about this branch of the Lutheran Church.

McGuinness, Margaret M. (2013). *Called to serve: A history of nuns in America*. New York: NYU Press.

Nadell, Pamela S. Rabbis in the United States. Jewish Women's Archive. http://jwa.org/encyclopedia/article/rabbis-in-united-states. Accessed 8/4/15.

Nesbitt, Paula D. (1997). *Feminization of the clergy In America: Occupational and organizational perspectives*. New York: Oxford University Press.

Owen-Towle, Carolyn S. (2011). Doors opened to women. UU World, May 16, 2011. http://www.uuworld.org/articles/women-uu-ministry.

Paulson, Michael (2007). Preaching fashion. The Boston Globe on Boston.com., February 18, 2007, http://www.boston.com.

Richardson-Moore, Deb (2012). *The weight of mercy: A novice pastor on the city streets.* Oxford, UK, and Grand Rapids, MI: Monarch Books.

Roman Catholic Womenpriests (2015). http://www.romancatholicwomenpriests.org/internationalmovement.

Roozen, David A. American Congregations 2010.http://faithcommunitiestoday.org/sites.

Schneider, Nathan (2015). New Monasticisms. TheRowBoat.com.

Sentilles, Sarah. (2008). *A church of her own: What happens when a woman takes the pulpit.* Orlando: Harcourt, Inc.

Smith, Christine A. (2013). *Beyond the stained glass ceiling.* Valley Forge, PA: Judson Press.

Tammeus, Bill (2014). Episcopal church celebrates 40 years of women in the priesthood. National Catholic Reporter, July 28, 2014.

Timeline of Women Rabbis (2015). http://us.wow.com/wiki/Timeline_of_women_rabbis.

UU Women's Federation (2015). http://www.uuwf.org.

Unitarian Universalist Association. http://www.uua.org/re/tapestry/adults.

United Church of Christ (2015). http://www.ucc.org/women.

Van Winkel, Jacinta (1993). Ladies of Bethany: A Letter to the Church of Pittsburgh.

Wesleyan-Holiness Women Clergy. http://www.whwomenclergy.org.

Zikmund, Barbara Brown; Lummis, Adair T.; & Chang, Patricia M.Y. (1998). *Clergy women: An uphill calling.* Louisville, KY: Westminster John Knox Press.